Grahame McLeod

# Makgadikgadi Pans

## A traveller's guide to the salt flats of Botswana

Published in 2019 by Struik Travel & Heritage
(an imprint of Penguin Random House South Africa (Pty) Ltd)
Reg. No. 1953/000441/07
The Estuaries No. 4, Oxbow Crescent,
Century Avenue, Century City, 7441
PO Box 1144, Cape Town, 8000 South Africa

www.penguinrandomhouse.co.za

10 9 8 7 6 5 4 3 2 1

**Publisher:** Pippa Parker
**Managing editor:** Roelien Theron
**Designer:** Gillian Black
**Cartographer:** Liezel Bohdanowicz
**Picture researcher:** Colette Stott
**Proofreader:** Thea Grobbelaar

Reproduction by Hirt & Carter Cape (Pty) Ltd
Printed and bound in China by Leo Paper Products Ltd.

9781775845577 (Print)
9781775845584 (ePub)

While every effort has been made to ensure that the information in this book was
correct at the time of going to press, some details might since have changed. The
author and publisher accept no responsibility for any inconvenience, loss, injury
or death sustained by any person using this book as a guide.

**Front cover:** Lekhubu Island (Maria Luisa Lopez Estivill/Dreamstime.com)
**Title page:** Wildebeest grazing in the lush grasslands near San Camp (Mike
Myers/Natural Selection)
**Back cover:** Herds of zebra and blue wildebeest in the Makgadikgadi and
Nxai Pans National Park (Martin Harvey/Natural Selection)

# Contents

Like dutiful sentries, the granitic monoliths of Lekhubu Island keep an eternal watch over the vast expanse of Sowa Pan.

The tar ended at Mmatshumo village, some 30 kilometres from the mining town of Letlhakane, itself a remote outpost in Botswana's Kalahari Desert. Here a sign pointed vaguely northwards to 'Lekhubu 45km'. I followed the sandy track through desolate mopane scrub for 5 kilometres to a lookout platform. From here, a strip of white was visible along the distant horizon. It was my first sighting of Sowa (sometimes spelt Sua) Pan, one of the two major salt flats that make up the Makgadikgadi Pans.

The track then zigzagged down towards the plains that surround the pans. For the next 9 kilometres, the terrain varied from hard calcrete to loose sand. I approached one of the many small pans dotted around Sowa. Here the track split into two and, with no signpost in sight, I took the right-hand one. For the first few kilometres all was well until I saw deep vehicle ruts ahead and a darkening of the pan surface. The wheels of the 4x4 began to spin. In the nick of time I made a U-turn and was able to escape the pan surface's wet clay. The thought of being stuck out here is not one to relish; I have heard of vehicles that have sunk down to their axles in the mud, or even disappeared entirely (the clay in the pans can reach a thickness of up to 100 metres), never to be seen again.

I returned to the junction and took the left-hand track across the same pan. The surface was hard and it did not take long to reach a veterinary fence, a little way beyond the pan's shoreline. The track continued through undulating grasslands to the edge of Sowa Pan, from where it was a final quick run of 17 kilometres across the white sea of salt to my destination – Lekhubu Island, its iconic rocky outcrops looming in the distance.

On the island I pitched camp in the shade of a pair of baobab trees – my idea of heaven. The dust in the air made for a great sunset and, as the evening wore on, the western sky changed from blue to shades of orange and red, and finally purple. After supper, the time had finally come to retreat to my camp bed. This served as a front-row seat for the nightly star show – a 360-degree view of thousands of stars that appeared as specks of ice in the jet-black sky.

This was not my first trip to Lekhubu Island, but it was the one that made me extend my wanderings around the Makgadikgadi, exploring not only the pans, but also the villages that skirt their perimeter, the Mosu/Kaitshe Escarpment with its spectacular views, the wild expanse of the Makgadikgadi and Nxai Pans National Park, and the lodges, inns and camp sites that cater for travellers seeking both solitude and adventure.

Each trip was a voyage of discovery, further revealing the complexities of the landscape's geological history, the vegetation that thrives in this semiarid region, the animals that have made this place their habitat and the people that have settled here.

From these excursions was born this book, a guide not only to the region's well-known wonders, but also to its hidden gems and its more remote past. I hope it will serve as a keepsake of a memorable and rewarding journey to this timeless place of peace, solitude and intense silence. In this vast expanse of salt, savanna and big open sky, you can truly gain another perspective on life.

## MAKGADIKGADI PANS MAP KEY

- • Town/village
- ✝ Airstrip
- ⚊ Camp site
- 🏠 Lodge
- ⛽ Filling station
- ⊠ Entrance gate
- Ⅴ Veterinary (vet) gate
- ⟊ 10 ⟊ Distance in kilometres
- —— Main/tarred road
- –·–·– Track (any vehicle)
- –––– Track (2x4 pickup truck/4x4)
- ····· Track (4X4 only)
- ⊢⊢⊢⊢ Railway
- ––––– Veterinary (vet) fence
- —— River
- ––––– Seasonal river
- ⊔⊔⊔⊔ Escarpment
- Pan
- Park
- **7** Chapter number

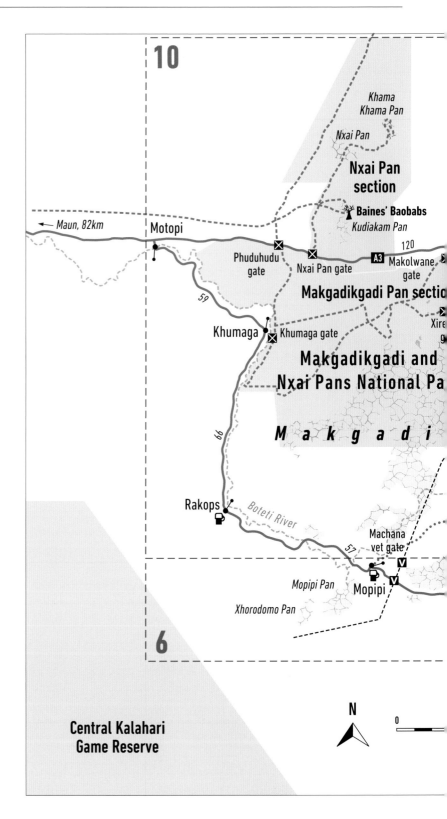

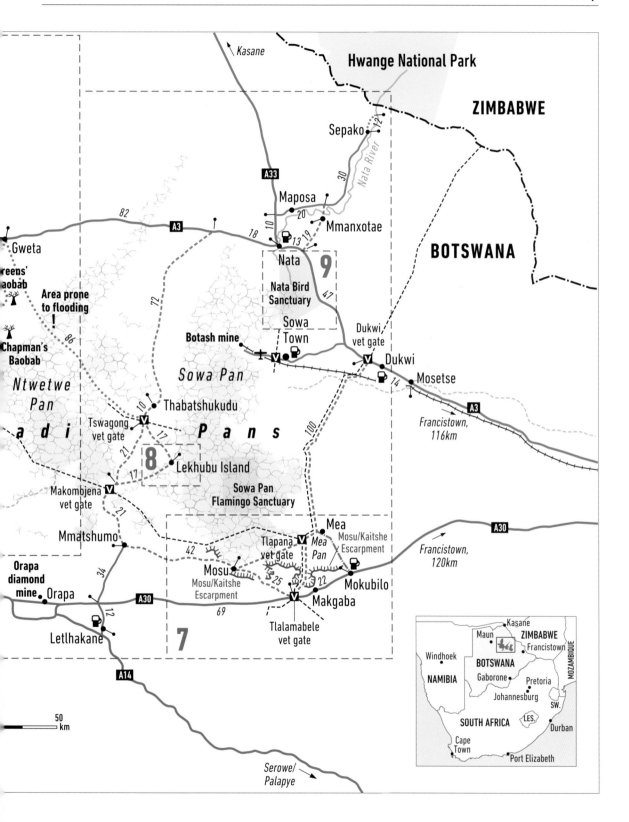

← Kasane

Hwange National Park

ZIMBABWE

Sepako

12

Nata River

30

A33

Maposa

20

BOTSWANA

Mmanxotae

82

A3

1

18

10

13 19

Gweta

reens'
aobab

Nata

9

Area prone
to flooding
!

72

Nata Bird
Sanctuary

47

Chapman's
Baobab

86

Sowa
Town

Dukwi
vet gate

Ntwetwe
Pan

Sowa Pan

Botash mine

V

Dukwi

Mosetse

14

adi

Thabatshukudu

10

Tswagong
vet gate

17

P a n s

100

A3

Francistown,
116km

21

8

Lekhubu Island

17

Sowa Pan
Flamingo Sanctuary

Makombjena
vet gate

V

Mea

A30

Mmatshumo

21

Tlapana
vet gate

V

Mea
Pan

Mosu/Kaitshe
Escarpment

Francistown,
120km

42

Orapa
diamond
mine

Orapa

34

Mosu

Mosu/Kaitshe
Escarpment

25

22

Mokubilo

A30

Makgaba

69

V

12

Letlhakane

7

Tlalamabele
vet gate

A14

50
km

Serowe/
Palapye →

Kasane

Maun

ZIMBABWE

Francistown

Windhoek

BOTSWANA

NAMIBIA

Gaborone

Pretoria

MOZAMBIQUE

Johannesburg

SW.

SOUTH AFRICA

LES.

Durban

Cape
Town

Port Elizabeth

# Introduction
## The Makgadikgadi Pans

## CHAPTER 1

JANDRIE LOMBARD/SHUTTERSTOCK

Although most visitors aim for the Okavango Delta and Chobe National Park, many now break their long journey at the Makgadikgadi Pans, an expanse of two large, irregularly shaped pans, Sowa and Ntwetwe, and an assortment of smaller salt and clay pans in Botswana's northeastern corner.

The pans cover a total area of over 12,000 square kilometres, making them one of the largest salt flats in the world. Ntwetwe and Sowa pans each exceed 100 kilometres in length, and at their widest points measure 80 and 50 kilometres, respectively. In fact, standing in the middle of either pan, you would see nothing about you but an endless canopy of blue sky and dazzling white plains extending to the distant horizon. To the visitor, accustomed to life in the concrete jungle, they may seem utterly devoid of life – but nothing could be further from the truth.

These dry salt lakes are the remains of a vast inland sea, Lake Makgadikgadi, that once covered an area of about 175,000 square kilometres. It was by all accounts one of the largest lakes on the African continent: ancient beaches, Stone Age tools and fossilized trees suggest that a more benign climate once prevailed here and that the conditions were suitable for both early humans and animals to subsist along the lake's shores. But even as temperatures rose and the lake dried up, humans continued to be drawn to the area. The stone remains of countless settlements along the southern fringes of Sowa Pan and the Mosu/Kaitshe Escarpment attest to the arrival of agropastoralists as early as the ninth century AD. While it is not entirely clear what attracted them, there is evidence that they would have participated in a regional trade network, exploiting and exchanging goods such as locally harvested salt for other items.

Today the region is one of extremes: for most of the year the pans are bone dry, lending the landscape an austere beauty. But when the summer rains arrive the region comes to life: the vegetation turns green once again, the grasses fringing the pans shoot to new heights, and birds and animals flock to water-filled pans.

Once covered with water, the ancient lakebed of the Makgadikgadi Pans is today hidden by layers of sand and salt.

DEVONJENKIN PHOTOGRAPHY/SHUTTERSTOCK

A greater flamingo spreads its wings in a display at Nata Bird Sanctuary at the northeastern end of Sowa Pan.

As the pans become inundated, millions of brine shrimp and other tiny crustaceans hatch from eggs that lay dormant in the saline sands during the dry months, drawing huge flocks of greater and lesser flamingo from places as far as East Africa and Namibia to feed, nest and breed in this remote corner of Botswana. Sowa Pan, in particular, is the continent's most important breeding site for the lesser flamingo. Nata Bird Sanctuary, at the northeastern end of the pan, was set up to protect these graceful creatures and a variety of other bird species.

The abundance of wildlife varies from season to season, with the dry season, from May to October, offering good opportunities for game viewing. Springbok, gemsbok, steenbok, giraffe and elephant, as well as predators such as leopard and lion, are all encountered here. A sight not to be missed though is Africa's second-biggest animal migration, triggered by the onset of the rainy season in December and January when thousands of blue wildebeest and zebra make their way from the Boteti River to Ntwetwe Pan to feed on the fresh grasses along the pan's margins.

## Best time to visit

Locals will say that any season is a good season for exploring the many moods of the Makgadikgadi Pans. However, it does make sense to get a handle on the weather when deciding on a travel itinerary.

The dry season, from May to October, is when game viewing is at its best. It is also easier to get around during this time of the year, as the tracks are likely to have dried out after the rains.

September and October are uncomfortably hot and dusty. But even these months bring unexpected gifts; this is when many trees, particularly the acacias, burst into flower, parading their white and yellow flowers at the most inhospitable time of year.

The rainy season, from November to March, is not as popular – mostly because the tracks across the pans and elswhere turn into a morass and become impassable. Nevertheless, these months have their own attractions. Towering cumulonimbus clouds darken the afternoon skies and short-lived downpours drench the desiccated landscape, bringing relief from the heat. Storm clouds give rise to spectacular sunsets, and lightning storms electrify the night. Spotting wildlife may be more difficult, however, as animals disperse over large areas to take advantage of bountiful grazing and pools of water.

SA-PICTURES/SHUTTERSTOCK

After particularly good rains, the salt-encrusted surface of the Makgadikgadi Pans disappears under a flood of water.

Another excellent spot for viewing game and watching birds is the Makgadikgadi and Nxai Pans National Park. A combination of salt and clay pans, flat areas of scrubland and rolling grasslands, it is home to a surprising variety and density of plains animals and their predators. Accommodation in and around the park ranges from rustic camp sites to luxurious lodges, all well appointed to take advantage of the spectacular scenery.

A number of towns and villages surround the pans. Although there are several options to choose from, many visitors use Nata as their gateway to Sowa Pan, staying either in lodges or camping at Nata Bird Sanctuary or on Lekhubu Island, well known for its huge baobab trees and ancient ruins from a long-gone era. Gweta offers access to Ntwetwe Pan as well as to the Makgadikgadi and Nxai Pans National Park to the west.

These are the mainstays in the area, but there are other, less well-known places tucked away around the perimeter of the pans. Settlements such as Mosu and Mmatshumo, at the southern end of Sowa Pan, and Mopipi, Rakops and Khamaga, along the western margins of Ntwetwe Pan, are doorways to the hidden gems of the region. Furthermore, along

with Nata and Gweta, many of these places are now hosts to an increasing number of activities and events – from organized camping safaris and 4x4 excursions to charity walks, quad biking, cycling and even land yachting. It is no wonder the region is slowly but surely growing as a popular tourism destination.

Getting around on the main roads is relatively straightforward. Sowa Pan is easily accessible, lying only a few kilometres from the tarred road (A3) between Francistown and Maun. Ntwetwe Pan can also be reached from the A3, but visiting its attractions means venturing off the beaten track via a dirt road from Zoroga or the old traders' route from Gweta.

Once you leave the tarred roads, you will definitely need an off-road vehicle. While saloon cars are fit for some dirt roads, a 4x4 or 2x4 pickup truck is essential if you want to explore the pans themselves or venture into more remote corners of the region.

However you choose to navigate these parts, whether by tar or off-road, you will find there is much to discover: under the vast blue sky are places of stark beauty, wide open spaces, rugged scenery, fascinating geological landforms, ancient ruins, and thriving plants, animals and birds. There is truly something for everyone.

# Geology
## Landscape of salt, sand and sea

## CHAPTER 2

First-time visitors to the Makgadikgadi Pans might be forgiven for thinking that only sand and salt exist here. But rocks do occur, invisible below the upper layers of sand and salt, or as rocky outcrops in an otherwise flat landscape. Even though these protruding rocks may be millions of years old, they are nevertheless very young compared to the granites and metamorphic rocks of the Basement Complex that underlie them and which probably date back more than 2,000 million years.

## Karoo System

The oldest rocks around the pans are those of the Karoo System (named after a semiarid region in South Africa where these rocks are best preserved). During the late Carboniferous to early Jurassic periods (300–180 million years ago), southern Africa formed part of the ancient supercontinent of Gondwanaland. This mega-sized landmass consisted of Africa, South America, India, Australia and much of Antarctica. During this time, a succession of sedimentary rocks – sandstones, shales, mudstones and siltstones – were deposited in layers, or beds, in rivers and lakes on a vast plain that extended over much of southern Africa. In Botswana, these sediments were deposited in the Kalahari Basin, a low-lying area flanked to the east and south by the Drakensberg and Cape mountain ranges, respectively, and to the west by the highlands of central Namibia.

Beginning with the oldest rocks, those making up the Karoo System – and where they can be seen in the Makgadikgadi region – are described here (see also Figure 1, p. 14).

### Mea arkose

This whitish, coarse-grained rock consists of quartz, plagioclase feldspar and small pebbles. It occurs in some areas along the eastern margin of Sowa Pan, especially around Mea Pan.

A white crust of salt, the remains of an inland sea, surrounds the rocky outcrop of Lekhubu Island.

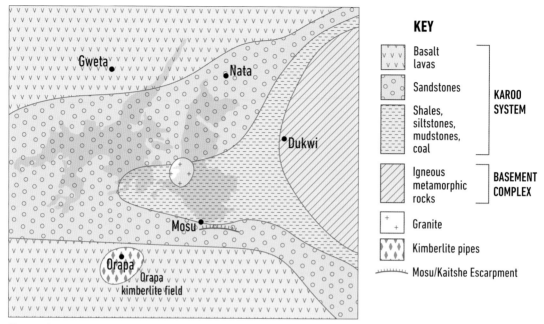

**KEY**

| | |
|---|---|
| Basalt lavas | |
| Sandstones | KAROO SYSTEM |
| Shales, siltstones, mudstones, coal | |
| Igneous metamorphic rocks | BASEMENT COMPLEX |
| Granite | |
| Kimberlite pipes | |
| Mosu/Kaitshe Escarpment | |

**Figure 1** Geological map of the Makgadikgadi region.

## Tlapana mudstone

This is a succession of mainly fine-grained grey, white and brownish mudstones and siltstones, which overlie the Mea arkose. The mudstone consists of clay minerals, such as kaolinite, together with quartz and feldspar. Whereas the siltstones consist of thin layers, mudstones are usually more massive in appearance. These rocks occur in areas bordering the southern margin of Sowa Pan to the east of Mosu village.

Petrified tree trunks, relics from a bygone forest, lie scattered along the southern edge of Sowa Pan, near Makgaba village.

Some of these mudstones are carbonaceous and were formed from the remains of vegetation. At the time these rocks were formed, about 280 million years ago, rainfall was higher than it is today and the vegetation probably consisted of swamp forests that included ferns and large trees such as conifers. When the trees died, they fell into the water where they decomposed and were rapidly buried under sediments. In time, they compacted to produce coal seams.

Fluids rich in silica also moved through these sediments and replaced the wood in a process known as petrification. The colour of petrified wood indicates the presence of specific elements. For example, iron oxides may give the wood a reddish-brown colour, while a blackish tint may be attributed to the presence of manganese oxides. Good examples of petrified trees are found a few kilometres to the east of the Tlalamabele veterinary gate, close to the Francistown–Orapa road. Although the internal structure and the original ribbing of the bark is still plain to see, the trees are now as hard as stone.

### Kautse beds

These beds include limestones, sandstones and siltstones. Unlike sandstones and siltstones, which were formed by deposition of sediments in rivers and lakes, the limestones were the result of chemical precipitation of the mineral calcite in clear, shallow water. The rocks that make up the Kautse beds occur between the Mosu/Kaitshe Escarpment and the southern margin of Sowa Pan.

### Mosu sandstone

This formation comprises a succession of medium- to coarse-grained, greyish sandstones, consisting mainly of quartz. Some of the sandstones are more reddish in colour due to the presence of iron oxides, such as hematite, which is present as a cement that binds the quartz grains together. The best place to see these rocks is at the Unikae Spring in Mosu village.

### Ntane sandstone

The youngest of the Karoo System rocks, Ntane sandstone was laid down in the Jurassic period when the climate became more desert-like. Strong winds eroded the sandstones that had formed there earlier on, producing sand grains which, when deposited, formed dunes. Over time, these dune sands turned into the hard, resistant Ntane sandstone that today caps the Mosu/Kaitshe Escarpment behind Mosu. The bedding in the sandstone shows that the winds blew in an east–west direction.

This sandstone is the same as the well-known orange-coloured Cave sandstone, visible throughout the lowlands of Lesotho and the Golden Gate Highlands National Park in the Free State of South Africa.

### Basalt lavas

About 180 million years ago, Gondwanaland broke up to produce the land masses that constitute today's continents. The event was accompanied by volcanic eruptions, with magma rising upwards from the earth's mantle along fractures in the existing rock and exiting at the surface as lava. The lava then cooled to form horizontal sheets of a fine-grained, blackish igneous rock, known as basalt.

Although basalt occurs over much of the pans area, it is usually buried under the more recent Kalahari beds. However, basalt outcrops are present in the vicinity of Orapa and Letlhakane, especially along streams.

## Granite

Lekhubu Island on Sowa Pan is made up of granite – a coarse-grained, greyish or pinkish rock. This igneous rock was formed by the cooling of large masses of magma, known as batholiths, deep below the surface. Large crystals are visible in the granite, suggesting that the magma cooled at a slow rate over a long period of time.

Erosion of the overlying rocks resulted in the granite being exposed at the surface. However,

Layers of Mosu sandstone appear at Unikae Spring in Mosu.

Lekhubu Island is composed of coarse-grained granite.

due to the presence of quartz, the granite itself is hard and thus fairly resistant to erosion, which explains why the island's granitic hillocks have not worn away over time.

## Kalahari beds

Soon after the breakup of Gondwanaland, much of Africa was occupied by three major low-lying areas, or drainage basins: the Chad Basin in the north, the Congo Basin in central Africa and the Kalahari Basin in the south. The Kalahari beds were laid down in the Kalahari Basin during the Tertiary and Quaternary periods (0–65 million years ago). They include the Kalahari sands, calcretes, silcretes and pan deposits.

### Kalahari sands

Around the pans, fine-grained greyish sands, consisting largely of quartz, were probably formed through wind erosion of the local Karoo sandstones. These were broken down to produce loose sand, deposited in vast flat sheets by the wind.

To the north of Sowa Pan and southwest of Ntwetwe Pan, long, narrow, east–west trending dunes occur. These were probably formed through the deposition of sand by strong easterly winds during an arid period about three million years ago. Barchan dunes (crescent-shaped, with their 'back' to the prevailing wind) may also be seen in this area.

Elsewhere in southern Africa, the Kalahari sands are more often reddish, yellow or orange in colour. The Kalahari sands make up the largest area of continuous sand in the world, covering an area of some 2,500,000 square kilometres from the Orange River in southern Africa to the forests of the Democratic Republic of the Congo.

### Calcrete

Layers of calcrete, or caliche, often occur in the Kalahari sands. Calcrete is found not only in southern Africa, but also in other semiarid and

Calcrete outcrops are visible in the bed of the Nata River.

arid regions of the world that receive an annual rainfall of less than 450 millimetres. Usually a cream-coloured rock, calcrete consists mainly of sand grains cemented together with calcium carbonate. It usually occurs as hard, massive sheet-like layers, known as hardpans, which lie horizontally and may be several metres thick.

In the Nata/Gweta area, calcrete occurs in sandy loam soil at a depth of only half a metre below the surface. Elsewhere, in the Orapa area, calcrete pebbles occur on the surface. In addition, a thick layer of calcrete caps the Mosu/Kaitshe Escarpment behind Mosu. Calcrete is also exposed in small cliffs along the margins of some pans. Here livestock utilize the calcrete as a mineral lick, as it contains calcium, a much-needed nutrient for teeth and bones.

Calcrete is used in road construction throughout the Kalahari. But beware: rainwater may cause the calcrete to dissolve, leaving potholes and corrugations in the road.

Calcrete, rich in calcium, serves as a mineral lick for cattle.

## Silcrete

Silcretes are sands that have been cemented by a compact, microcrystalline (very fine-grained), hard, flint-like form of silica known as chalcedony. Like flint, it breaks to produce a smooth fracture in the shape of a scallop shell. Although they are usually black in colour, silcretes can assume a wide range of hues, including cream, brown and white, while the presence of the mineral glauconite usually gives them a greenish tone. Silcrete is often exposed on the floors of pans, especially along their margins.

Stone Age humans used silcrete to make primitive tools such as arrowheads and scrapers.

## Pan formation

Many of the smaller pans were formed in the last five million years and are much younger in age than the rocks of the Karoo System (see Figure 2, below). Some geologists suggest that they were formed by deflation, a type of wind erosion that blows away loose layers of sand on the surface of a flat expanse of land, thereby producing shallow depressions, or pans. In the Makgadikgadi, the prevailing northeasterly winds deposited the loose sand in the shape of small crescent-shaped barchan dunes, discernable at Rysana Pan and in the Kedia Hill area, both near Mopipi. It is estimated that these dunes were formed over the last 60,000 years.

The silcrete (above left) on the Sowa Pan floor is darker in colour than that along the Boteti River (above right).

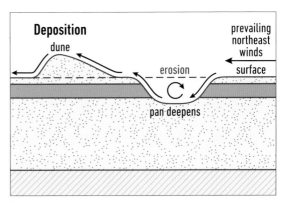

**Figure 2** Diagram illustrating how pans and barchan dunes are formed through the processes of deflation and deposition.

However, subsequent major geological events played a much more significant role in the formation of today's Makgadikgadi salt pans.

## Lake Makgadikgadi

### Formation of the lake

About five million years ago, wind erosion further lowered the land surface in northern Botswana to produce a large natural depression. Geologists believe that earth movements along faults also contributed to creating this feature. At this time, the Chobe River, together with the Okavango and Zambezi rivers, flowed southeastwards to form the proto-Limpopo River. This 'super river' most likely flowed along the course of today's Motloutse River in eastern Botswana. It appears to have carried vast volumes of water, as the Motloutse is substantially wider than the Limpopo into which it flows in the Tuli Block at Botswana's eastern border with Zimbabwe and South Africa (see Figure 3A, above).

However, some two million years ago, an uplift of the earth's crust in eastern Botswana produced an area of higher land (known as the Zimbabwe–Kalahari Axis), which resulted in the damming of the three rivers and the

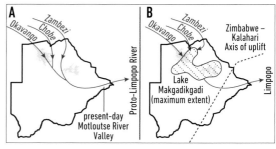

**Figure 3** The proto-Limpopo River drainage basin (**A**); The Zimbabwe–Kalahari Axis, which dammed the rivers of the drainage basin to form Lake Makgadikgadi (**B**).

formation of a giant inland sea, known as Lake Makgadikgadi (see Figure 3B, above). These rivers, together with others that flowed into the lake, such as the Lepashe, Mosetse, Semowane, Nata and Okwa, deposited fine sands and greenish or black clays (up to a thickness of 200 metres) in the lake. The thickness of the deposits indicates that the sediments must have accumulated gradually over thousands of years.

Waves crashing on the lake's shoreline deposited coarse sand, gravel and well-rounded pebbles to form beaches. Fossil beaches of rounded pebbles may be seen at Lekhubu Island and at the base of the Mosu/Kaitshe Escarpment. Elsewhere along the shoreline, finer sand was deposited in the form of ridges,

**Figure 4** Land map showing the most conspicuous landforms around the Makgadikgadi Pans.

The Gidikwe Sand Ridge rises sharply from the surrounding plains. Inset: The Nata–Maun road cuts through the ridge between the villages of Phuduhudu and Motopi.

some of which are several metres in height. One example can be found at the southern end of present-day Lake Ngami in northwestern Botswana. Another example is the Magwikhwe Ridge – some 100 kilometres long by 200 metres wide – which rises about 20 metres above the surrounding plains. The track that leads from the Moremi Game Reserve's North gate to Savuti Camp in the Chobe National Park crosses this sandy ridge.

Offshore bars – linear sand ridges formed when breaking waves shed their load – were also deposited in Lake Makgadikgadi, parallel to the shore. Between the bars and the shoreline were shallow lagoons. One example of an offshore bar is Gidikwe Sand Ridge, a north–south landform that once marked the western margin of the palaeo-lake. Where it crosses the Nata–Maun road, between the villages of Phuduhudu and Motopi, the road cuts through the sandy ridge (see Figure 4, opposite page). From here there is a short off-ramp leading to a lookout point on the summit, which affords spectacular views over the old lakebed to the east and the ridge of sand stretching to the north and south.

Spits, like offshore bars, are linear deposits of sand, but are joined to the shore at one end. A good example can be seen at the Botswana

Ash (Botash) salt processing plant where a spit runs in a northwesterly direction for several kilometres out into Sowa Pan.

Old shorelines, marked by beach deposits, show variations in the levels of the lake as it grew in size and retreated at different times. The most conspicuous shorelines occur at altitudes of 912, 920, 936, 940 and 945 metres above sea level – these represent periods when the lake levels remained constant for long stretches of time, making it possible for beaches to form. Given that the lowest point at Sowa Pan today is 890 metres, the greatest depth of the lake must have been at least 55 metres. At its greatest extent, the lake probably covered an area up to 175,000 square kilometres, extending between the pans in the east to as far as the panhandle of the Okavango Delta in the west. It seems likely that the lake reached its greatest extent some 50,000 years ago, but even as recently as 20,000 years ago, the lake was filled to capacity.

Where did all the water come from? The Okavango Delta is one likely source – after all, today it accounts for 95 per cent of Botswana's surface water. The average volume of water carried by the Okavango River from Angola to the delta each year is about 11 cubic kilometres. Rainfall contributes a further 3.2 cubic kilometres, bringing the total yearly accumulation of water in the delta to almost 15 cubic kilometres – although much of it is usually lost through evaporation. The Chobe River is a much smaller river than the Okavango: its average annual flow amounts to only 3 cubic kilometres. Combined, these two rivers could not have sustained a body of water as large as Lake Makgadikgadi. Bearing this in mind, it seems more probable that much of Makgadikgadi's water was supplied by the upper Zambezi River, which today has an average flow of 40 cubic kilometres. It is thus likely that all three rivers flowed into the ancient lake.

Scientists also believe that rainfall in the area was higher in the past. Cycles of high and low rainfall have been occurring over the last 200,000 years, with each cycle lasting about 23,000 years. During the high rainfall periods, precipitation may have exceeded 900 millimetres, about double the rainfall today. Such periods usually resulted in higher water levels.

The names of some of the places and villages around the Makgadikgadi Pans also suggest that a lake, as well as abundant wildlife, once existed here. For example, in Setswana, *Letlhakane*, the name of a mining town, means 'reeds'; *Kubu* (or *Lekhubu*), the name of a rock island in Sowa Pan, means 'hippo'; and *Thabatshukudu*, a cattle post, means 'hill of the rhinoceros'.

## Drying up of the lake

Why then did this 'super lake' disappear? A clue lies in the name of the pans: Makgadikgadi comes from the Setswana word *go kgala*, which means 'to dry up', and that is exactly what happened.

The desiccation of the lake was the result of a complex process involving several factors. When Lake Makgadikgadi first formed, the Okavango Delta probably did not exist, and so the Okavango River, together with the Chobe and Zambezi rivers, was able to flow southeastwards, draining into the mega-lake without interruption. Tectonic activity, the development of several northeast–southwest trending faults, and climate change all may have played a role in causing the lake to peter out.

These faults seemed to have developed no more than 120,000 years ago. As the earth's

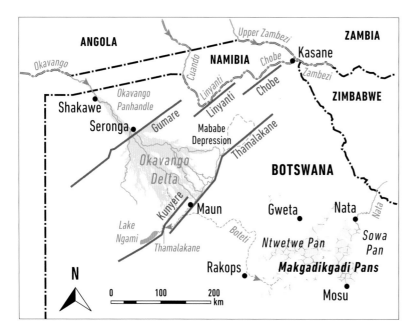

**Figure 5** Land map showing the extension of the East African Rift Valley in Botswana. The northeast–southwest trending faults that form part of the rift valley stemmed the flow of the Okavango, Chobe and Zambezi rivers into Lake Makgadikdadi.

crust tore apart, earth movements caused land between the Thamalakane, Kunyere and Gumare faults in northern Botswana to slide downwards to form a small rift valley, an extension of the great East African Rift Valley. Low cliffs formed along the sides of the valley, preventing the Okavango River from flowing southwards and serving as a 'wall' behind which the river was dammed to create the Okavango Delta. At the same time, the flow of the Chobe and Zambezi rivers was redirected eastwards along the Linyanti and Chobe faults at the northern end of the rift valley. This caused the Chobe to flow into the Zambezi, which itself was diverted eastwards towards the Indian Ocean. No longer fed by these rivers, the ancient lake gradually evaporated and dried up (see Figure 5, opposite page). As the lake emptied, salts – common salt (sodium chloride) and soda ash (sodium carbonate) – were precipitated from the water, leaving behind the vast white expanse that characterizes the network of pans in northern Botswana today.

A section of the rift valley cliffs is visible on the road from Francistown to Maun. In Maun, shortly before reaching the Thamalakane River, the road drops by about ten metres – the cliff here marks the position of the Thamalakane fault.

Climate change might also have contributed to the eventual disappearance of the 'super

## Africa's great rift valley

Geologists believe that the Okavango Delta forms the southwestern extension of the great East African Rift Valley. This long, linear lowland feature, bordered by higher areas, stretches over 6,000 kilometres, from Jordan in the Middle East, along the length of the Red Sea and eastern Africa, to the mouth of the Zambezi River in Mozambique. One smaller branch of the rift valley runs along part of the Zambezi River, where it forms the border between Zambia and Zimbabwe, and then extends in a southwesterly direction to include the Okavango Delta.

The Western Rift, also called the Albertine Rift, includes many of the African Great Lakes. The Western Rift is one of the most biodiverse regions in Africa, featuring a narrow corridor of highland forests, snow-capped mountains, savannas and chains of lakes and wetlands. Lake Tanganyika, whose long shores are shared by Burundi, the Democratic Republic of the Congo, Tanzania and Zambia, is the largest of the rift valley lakes. It is also the second-deepest and second-biggest (by volume of fresh water) lake in the world. Only Lake Baikal is deeper and holds more water. Like many freshwater rift valley lakes, Lake Tanganyika is home to hundreds of endemic species of cichlid fish.

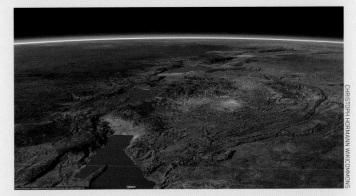

A computer rendering of the western arm of the East African Rift Valley shows (from top to bottom) the Albert, Edward, Kivu and Tanganyika lakes.

CHRISTOPH HORMANN WIKICOMMONS

Permanent water pools in the Nata River attract birds and other wildlife throughout the seasons.

lake'. About 20,000 years ago, a hotter and drier period set in, which resulted in an increase in evaporation and a decrease in both rainfall and the volume of water flowing into the lake. By 10,000 years ago, the volume of water held in the lake had diminished substantially. Lake levels still fluctuated though, and scientists believe that the lake reached the 912-metre level on a number of occasions during this time. John Cooke, a leading Botswana geomorphologist, suggests that as recently as 500 years ago rainfall may still have been much higher than at present. Even if the lake had already disappeared by then, the pans may have still been a vast wetland, similar to today's Okavango Delta.

Had faulting not occurred, it is still likely that the ancient lake would have dried up. Scientists have shown that high rates of evaporation associated with a drier climate can greatly affect the water levels of rivers. Today, of the water that flows into the Okavango Delta at the village of Seronga in years of high rainfall, a staggering 96 per cent is lost by evaporation before the water even reaches Maun further downstream. Based on this evidence, the inflow of the Okavango

River into the lake during warmer times would have been much less than the volume of water lost by evaporation. This would have led to a fall in water levels in the lake, causing it eventually to disappear.

**The pans today**

Today the climate is dry and, in most years, there is no water in the pans. But in years of good rainfall, the Nata River, which has its source near Bulawayo in Zimbabwe, may empty large amounts of water into the northern part of Sowa Pan. Smaller amounts of water may also be carried into the pan from the east by the Lepashe, Mosetse, Mosope and Semowane rivers. Estimates indicate that, at a mean annual rainfall of 450 millimetres, the pans receive an average of 3.6 cubic kilometres of water from rainfall alone each year. In addition, an annual average of 0.166 cubic kilometres of water flows from the five rivers mentioned above into Sowa Pan. Of this, the Nata River contributes 0.136 cubic kilometres. Discharged groundwater may be another source of water in the pans.

All these rivers have their source along a major watershed, the Zimbabwe–Kalahari

Axis, which runs from north to south in eastern Botswana and extends into Zimbabwe. Here the annual rainfall is higher than at the pans. For instance, Francistown in eastern Botswana receives 500 millimetres of rain per year and the area around Bulawayo in Zimbabwe gets more than 600 millimetres.

When Sowa Pan becomes inundated, in windy conditions whitecaps and waves can be seen breaking along the northern shore. However, this inland sea is usually very shallow and the water is less than knee-deep – a distant shadow of the giant lake that once existed here.

In 2017, though, things were a little different: large areas of Sowa Pan were flooded and the depth of water exceeded 4 metres in places.

In contrast, Ntwetwe Pan is less subject to flooding. The main reason for this is that only one major river, the Boteti, reaches the pan. This river receives much of its water from the distant Okavango and the flow rarely extends along its entire 300-kilometre length to discharge water into the southwestern corner of the pan. A notable wet spot has recently been identified in the southeast corner of the pan, probably created by the discharge of groundwater.

## Features on the pan surface

When a pan dries out after flooding, a thin hard film of white salt is left behind, and a number of short-lived features usually develop on the surface. Salt blisters form due to the peeling of the salt layer into very thin sheets. Cracks may also appear in the shape of polygons, each one measuring about 50 centimetres across. Their margins bend upwards to form low ridges a few centimetres in height.

Once the pans are flooded again, these features disintegrate, only for the cycle to repeat itself as the water evaporates in the heat of summer.

Salt crystals form on the surface of the pan after flooding.

Salt blisters appear as the salt layer begins to dry out.

Cracks on the pan's surface take the shape of polygons.

# Climate

## Seasons of extremes

## CHAPTER 3

Due to the country's low altitude and the location of the Makgadikgadi Pans in the centre of southern Africa, far from the oceans, the region has a warm, subtropical, semiarid climate. The weather conditions are nevertheless variable and are likely to differ between seasons and from year to year. As no two years are the same, the visitor must be well prepared for any type of weather.

## Rainfall

### Amount of rain

Rainfall for the Makgadikgadi area is generally low, averaging around 400–450 millimetres per annum. Rain here typically falls in short heavy showers and is usually accompanied by thunder, lightning and, on occasion, hail. Such heavy rain can come suddenly, without warning. A summer's morning may dawn like any other, bright and clear, with only a few puffy white cumulus clouds appearing around midday to alert you to a possible deluge in the late afternoon.

All too quickly, though, masses of hot air, or convection currents, transform these harmless-looking clouds into towering cumulonimbus clouds. You might be forgiven for thinking that the raindrops will quickly evaporate in the searing heat before they reach the ground. Instead, the clouds darken, the wind strengthens, lightning streaks across the sky and thunder rumbles through the air to announce the arrival of the first drops of rain. The rain soon gathers momentum and in no time only a faint outline of the landscape can be seen through a curtain of falling water. Dried-up riverbeds around the pans suddenly come back to life as torrents of coffee-coloured water race along them, uprooting bushes and trees in their path.

A dramatic sunset follows a brief downpour of rain over Sowa Pan during a summer thunderstorm.

HIROMI ITO AME/SHUTTERSTOCK

A rainbow illuminates the dark sky at Nata Lodge after a storm.

quickly turn into a sodden morass a few hours later. Under such conditions, even robust 4x4 vehicles will get stuck and sink down to their axles, or even disappear! A winch will be of little use here since there are no trees to which it can be attached.

### Seasonality and variability

Although the area is hot and dry for much of the year, there is a rainy season, which occurs in the summer months, from November to March.

Nevertheless, rainfall varies from one year to the next: in good years the rain arrives in October and continues into April or even May, but in poor years the rainy season is much shorter, beginning in late December and ending in February. In such years, dry spells, accompanied by clear skies, occur intermittently, and can last for several days or weeks.

The winter months, from May to August, are normally dry, but heavy rains have been recorded for this time of year: in June 2010, 194 millimetres of rain fell over Nata in just two days, causing flooding in the area.

More extreme weather events do occur as well, and may have a severe impact on people and businesses at the local level. A staggering 368 millimetres – about 75 per cent of the average annual rainfall – fell at Nata in January 2008 alone. The torrential rains resulted in the flooding of Nata Lodge, forcing it to close for several weeks. Heavy rains and flooding also caused the lodge to shut down in February 2014 and, again, in February/March 2017. If you plan to visit the pans in the rainy season, phone ahead to make sure your chalet has not turned into an island that can only be reached by a *mokoro*.

A mass of water may flood the pans, rapidly transforming them into temporary lakes. Then, suddenly, it is all over; the sun breaks through and the clouds dissipate to reveal yet another stunning sunset, as if nothing extraordinary had happened at all during the day.

If you are out on the pans, watch the weather and, if necessary, make sure that you have sufficient time to get off the pans before the rains begin. A dry pan in the morning may

## Temperature

Seasonal extremes and variable temperatures are an inescapable part of life around the pans. Here there are three distinct dry seasons – cool, hot and warm – and a hot wet season.

## Cool dry season

May to August is the cool dry season, with pleasant warm days (23–25⁰C) and cool to cold nights (5–8⁰C). The difference between day and night temperatures is greatest at this time of year – at night, winter woollies and gloves are a must, but around midday shirtsleeves are called for. Since the skies are usually clear of cloud, temperatures rise rapidly during the day, but plummet once the sun has gone down.

Sometimes a strong cold front may push far inland over the interior of southern Africa. But, by the time it reaches Botswana, it has usually lost all its moisture with no chance of rainfall. Behind the cold front, temperatures may plummet to between 0 and -5°C, with frost conditions prevailing. At such times the winds blow from the southwest, and even at midday the air may feel distinctly chilly. Yet the days are clear, marked by vivid blue skies free of haze and dust, making this the best time for photography.

You can easily predict the arrival of a cold front by simply observing the weather. Before the cold arrives, temperatures may be relatively high (25–30°C), accompanied by northwesterly winds and partly cloudy skies. The arrival of the cold front is announced by strong southwesterly winds – the stronger the front, the stronger the winds and the longer they will blow before dying down. Once the winds have abated, the temperatures will plummet. Don't be surprised if you see frozen water in your pots in the early morning!

## Hot dry season

September and October make up the hot dry season. Temperatures rise rapidly in early September, with daytime temperatures often exceeding 35°C from the middle of the month onward. The highest day temperatures, up to 40°C, usually occur in October. The heat is somewhat tempered by the low levels of humidity experienced during this season.

# Veld fires

If good rains fall during the previous year's rainy season, the pans will be fringed by an abundance of grass that, when dry, is vulnerable to fire. If a fire does break out during the hot summer months, strong winds may exacerbate the situation, causing the fire to race uncontrollably across the dry grasslands and damage property.

Although they may wreak havoc, fires are also beneficial to the grasslands: the ash adds valuable nutrients, such as calcium, to the soil, thereby encouraging the rapid growth of fresh green grass once the rains begin. In addition, the seeds of some plants require the intense heat of a fire before germination can take place.

Although grasses may benefit from fires, trees and bushes are less well adapted to conflagration. Most trees and bushes less than 2 metres in height will be destroyed by a veld fire, but those taller than 2 metres have a better chance of survival and may even regrow or coppice.

Runaway veld fires in the dry season burn everything in their path.

**27**

# Cyclone Dineo – a rare weather event

The 2016/17 rainy season at the pans was characterized by unusually heavy rainfall, courtesy of a La Niña weather event, which brought with it cooler weather and well above average rainfall.

Trees uprooted during a flood lie piled up next to a bridge over the Nata River.

In mid-February 2017, the area also received a rare and unwelcome visitor – the tropical cyclone Dineo. Tropical cyclones originate over the warm waters of the Indian Ocean and are fairly common in Mozambique between January and March most years. Although these may subside quickly as they move further west inland, unusually Dineo reached as far as Botswana.

The cyclone was accompanied by daily rainfall in excess of 100 millimetres and widespread flooding. In Nata village, the Nata River overflowed its banks, completely submerging the bridge. East of the village, the Francistown road was under water for several kilometres. Much of the river's water was discharged into the northern end of Sowa Pan, inundating the salt flat for a distance of more than 20 kilometres from the shoreline.

For several weeks the road between Nata and Gweta was under water, and Gweta village, north of the pans, was declared a disaster zone. But every cloud has a silver lining, and an entrepreneur in Gweta used a flatbed truck to carry small cars and tow larger vehicles some 3 kilometres over a particularly bad section of flooded road.

Roads near Gweta disappeared under pools of water as heavy rains brought on by Cyclone Dineo caused severe flooding.

Dust devils racing across Sowa Pan are a common feature in the dry season.

### Hot wet season

During the hot wet season, from November to March, day temperatures may fall a few degrees, with readings seldom exceeding 35°C. In fact, in wet years some days may feel rather chilly, as cloudy conditions prevail and temperatures fail to rise above 20°C.

### Warm dry season

The month of April is autumn at the pans. The weather is generally warm and dry at this time, with day temperatures of 28–30°C, and the landscape is likely still to be fresh and green after the rains.

## Winds

Most visitors may think that the wind never stops blowing at the pans. One reason for the incessant wind is that the land here is flat, with few trees to break the speed of the wind.

Most of the year the winds are light and blow from the east or northeast, but in August and September, when they blow from the northwest, they are stronger and usually hot and dry. If you are camping during these months, ensure that your tent is well secured – if it does take off, accept that you may never see it again. As the air is often hazy and laden with dust at this time of the year, be sure to protect your camera if you are out taking photographs – the finest of particles can affect your equipment. And remember to drink plenty of fluids on these dry, hot days.

During the dry and dusty months, small whirlwinds, or dust devils, can be seen racing across the dry surface of the pans. This small-scale version of a tornado forms as hot, light air rapidly rises from the pan's surface through a layer of cooler air. The hot air begins to rotate, carrying dust with it as it circles upwards. When the source of hot air becomes exhausted, the surrounding cooler air is sucked in, resulting in the dust devil dissipating in just a few seconds. These miniature whirlwinds are quite harmless, so don't expect yourself, or your vehicle, to be suddenly lifted off the ground or go into orbit. Nevertheless, keep your hands firmly on the steering wheel should a dust devil cross your path.

# Vegetation and wildlife

## A system of mutual dependence

## CHAPTER 4

An occasional oasis, the Makgadikgadi Pans sprawl across the centre of the Kalahari Basin, the largest expanse of continuous sand in the world, stretching from the Orange River along the South African border to the Democratic Republic of the Congo in central Africa. Plants and animals coexist in this finely balanced ecosystem, the trees, shrubs and grasses providing shelter and food for all manner of animals, whose behaviours, in turn, create the necessary conditions for the vegetation to thrive. It is the interconnectedness of all living things in an ostensibly barren landscape that makes the Makgadikgadi Pans such a fascinating destination.

## Plant life

The pans are considered by most people to form an integral part of the Kalahari Desert. The term 'desert' is, however, a misnomer – even though the area is covered by deep, loose sand, the Kalahari is not a true desert. It receives a fair amount of annual rainfall, with the result that it lacks the extreme aridity of deserts such as the Namib or Sahara. And unlike these deserts, the Kalahari, and much of Botswana, is relatively well vegetated, with a mixture of grasses and trees that are typical of the savanna biome surviving in conditions of relative aridity.

### Vegetation types

A range of vegetation types can be identified around the salt pans, the result of variable factors such as geology, topography, soil type and water supply. By paying close attention to variations in the type, size, height and density of the plants, as well as their leaves, flowers and fruits, the traveller may well be able to identify the region's main vegetation types and their representative species (see Figure 1, p. 32).

### Halophytic vegetation

Conditions on the salt pans are harsh, and trees and large bushes are absent from this environment. The saline nature of the soil means that only halophytic species – plants that grow

COLIN BELL / NATURAL SELECTION

Hundreds of zebra and blue wildebeest graze on the plains around Ntwetwe Pan, attracted by the succulent grasses that grow here in the wake of the summer rains.

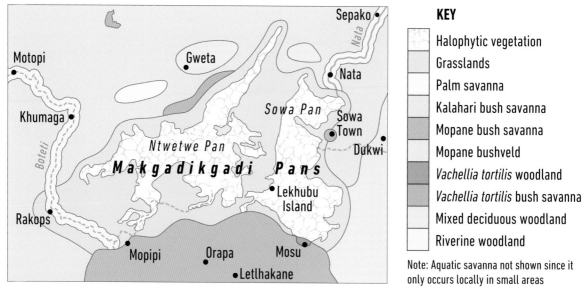

KEY

| | |
|---|---|
| | Halophytic vegetation |
| | Grasslands |
| | Palm savanna |
| | Kalahari bush savanna |
| | Mopane bush savanna |
| | Mopane bushveld |
| | *Vachellia tortilis* woodland |
| | *Vachellia tortilis* bush savanna |
| | Mixed deciduous woodland |
| | Riverine woodland |

Note: Aquatic savanna not shown since it only occurs locally in small areas

**Figure 1** The vegetation types of the Makgadikgadi region.

Saltbush is commonly found along the pan margins.

The cactus-like hoodia flowers in winter. Its large, maroon flowers mimic the smell of decaying meat (left). An iconic grasslands species, the mopane aloe produces red flowers in winter (right).

in conditions of high salinity – can take root here, and then mostly only along the pan margins. The plants have a stunted, low growth habit, their height being kept in check by the salt content in the soil.

Waterlogging also plays a role in discouraging plant growth on the pans. During good rainfall years, the water builds up in the clay soil, with nowhere to drain away. As the water infiltrates all the air spaces, it robs the soil of oxygen, making it impossible for roots to grow.

The main species found here is saltbush (*Salsola rabieana*), a succulent creeping plant with small swollen leaves.

**Grassland**

Open grasslands occur on slightly raised ground adjacent to and between the pans. The soils are mainly greyish in colour and are less saline than those on the pans. The grasslands may also be seasonally flooded, usually only for short periods of time.

Although the vegetation consists predominantly of a few hardy grass species, such as the saline-resistant prickly salt grass (*Odyssea paucinervis*), some succulents grow here, too. The cactus-like hoodia (*Hoodia lugardii*) and the single-stemmed mopane aloe (*Aloe littoralis*) are typical grassland species.

The real fan palm tree is synonymous with the Makgadikgadi Pans and the Okavango Delta.

## Palm savanna

Palm trees punctuate the landscape north of Ntwetwe Pan, approximately 50 kilometres west of Gweta. Stands of these trees also grow in Nata village and around the springs at Mosu.

The dominant species is the real fan palm (*Hyphaene petersiana*), known as *mokolwane*. It has large fan-shaped leaves with leafstalks armed with black, hooked thorns. The tree produces large reddish-brown edible fruits that are enjoyed by elephants and baboons, as well as humans.

## Kalahari bush savanna

Various thorn tree species are closely associated with the Kalahari bush savanna. The most distinctive is the camel thorn (*Vachellia erioloba*). A medium-sized tree, with long, straight, white thorns and yellow, ball-shaped flowers, this species grows as a multistemmed shrub in the Makgadikgadi area. Another thorny species is the candlepod acacia (*Vachellia hebeclada*), a sprawling bush common in areas underlain by calcrete. Its hooked thorns are straight, white and

Candlepod acacia is a low spreading shrub, characterized by a conspicuous crown.

paired, and are shorter than those of the camel thorn. It has upright pods, which distinguish it from other *Vachellia* species where the pods hang downwards. The black thorn (*Senegalia mellifera*) has short, hooked paired thorns and bears white, ball-shaped flowers.

Non-thorny species include the Kalahari apple-leaf (*Philenoptera nelsii*), which grows in areas of very deep, loose sand, especially to the west of Gweta. The silver terminalia (*Terminalia sericea*), with its silver-grey leaves, spike-like, white flowers and pinkish papery fruits, is common throughout the Kalahari.

Grass species include giant three-awned grass (*Aristida meridionalis*) and silky Bushman grass (*Stipagrostis uniplumis*).

Silky Bushman grass is one of the dominant grass species in the Kalahari bush savanna.

# Survival mechanisms of savanna plants and trees

The baobab is the world's largest succulent.

Plants in the Makgadikgadi region do not have much going for them; life here is tough, a never-ending struggle for survival against searing summer heat, lack of water, strong winds, and poor sandy or saline soils. If that is not enough, there are plenty of herbivores – both livestock and wildlife – that can't resist making a meal of them. Despite these harsh conditions, the plants that survive here have adapted in a variety of ways to ensure their continued existence.

Many plants are able to maximize the amount of water that they can absorb from the soil. Some, like baobab or camel thorn trees, have deep extensive root systems that enable them to draw up water and food from deep underground. Others have shallow roots, but spread over a large area just below the surface to help the plant take in moisture from dew or light showers. Plants with such root systems usually grow far apart to avoid competition for water.

Other plants have developed strategies to minimize water loss. For example, mopane trees are deciduous and simply shed their leaves during the dry season – it is through the leaves that plants lose precious water to the atmosphere. The leaves of mopane trees also hang downwards during the day, which reduces the surface area exposed directly to

Camel thorn trees are widely spaced to minimize competition for water, a scarce resource in savannas.

The butterfly-shaped leaves of the mopane tree hang downwards during the heat of the day.

the sun. Acacia trees have very small leaves, thus providing a much smaller surface area for the loss of water through transpiration.

Grasses, too, protect themselves during the dry season. Although their leaves may turn yellow and die back at this time, their roots are still alive, although dormant. With the onset of the rainy season, nutrients stored in the roots are used by the plant to produce new shoots.

Succulents are uniquely adapted to retain water in their tissues following periods of heavy or prolonged rainfall. The largest succulent of them all, the baobab can hoard thousands of litres of moisture in its thick, fleshy stem. The saltbush, found along the pans, stores water in its small swollen leaves. A few species, such as prickly salt grass, can survive in saline soils because they are able to excrete salt from the water that they have absorbed. The salt exits the leaves through the stomata; such leaves may be covered with salt crystals.

Acacia plants produce closely spaced thorns along their branches to limit the number of leaves eaten by herbivores. Giraffes and the ubiquitous goats, however, have a tough leathery tongue that enables them to access sufficient quantities of the small leaves.

Growing up to a height of 2 metres, the giant three-awned grass is the tallest grass species in the area.

A vigorous creeper, prickly salt grass grows along the verges of the pans.

The umbrella thorn has tiny leaves and sharp thorns.

CHRIS FOURIE/SHUTTERSTOCK

A giraffe feeds on the leaves of an umbrella thorn tree.

## Mopane bush savanna

This vegetation type is conspicuous south of the pans around Letlhakane, Orapa and Mopipi; in Nata; and in the countryside between Sowa Town and the Francistown–Maun road. Soils in these areas are calcareous and often contain a layer of hard calcrete just below the surface. This restricts root development and curbs the growth of large trees.

One of the most recognizable species in southern Africa, the mopane (*Colophospermum mopane*) can grow up to 30 metres in areas where there is ample water and favourable soil conditions. In the dry Makgadikgadi region, it grows as a multistemmed bush, reaching a height of only up to 5 metres. In late autumn, its distinctive butterfly-shaped leaves turn reddish brown, and in early summer the new leaves have an attractive reddish colour before they turn

The purplepod clusterleaf displays its attractive plum-red pods for much of the year.

green. The only other common species here is the purplepod clusterleaf (*Terminalia prunioides*), identifiable by its spike-like, cream-white flowers and attractive plum-red papery pods.

## Mopane bushveld

Unlike mopane bush savanna, this vegetation type supports a wide variety of both trees and bushes. It is associated with firmer reddish-brown loam soils and occurs in the area between Francistown and the turnoff to Sowa Pan. The trees that make up this vegetation include mopane, knob thorn (*Senegalia nigrescens*), marula (*Sclerocarya birrea*) and several *Vachellia* species. Common bush species are sickle bush (*Dichrostachys cinerea*), which produces sharp spines and curly, twisted pods, and several *Grewia* species, identified by their small reddish-brown edible fruits.

## *Vachellia tortilis* woodland

A drought-resistant species, umbrella thorn (*Vachellia tortilis*), with its characteristic mix of long, straight, white thorns and short, hooked ones, grows in loam soils. It can endure high temperatures and alkaline environments, and is more tolerant of flooding than other species.

Stands of large, densely spaced umbrella thorns, along with bushveld albizia (*Albizia harveyi*), can be seen in the village of Mosu.

One of southern Africa's best-known indigenous trees, the mopane grows as a multistemmed bush in the Makgadikgadi region.

The umbrella thorn is common in Mosu village, where it is referred to by locals as the *mosu* tree.

The bushveld albizia produces long, narrow, flattened pods.

The growth of such large trees is due to the presence of deep loam soils, as opposed to the less fertile sandy soils that occur over much of the surrounding area. The umbrella thorn bears white, ball-shaped flowers and narrow, twisted pale brown pods, whereas the bushveld albizia produces fluffy white flowers with long stamens and flat, narrow pods that are brown in colour.

### *Vachellia tortilis* bush savanna

This savanna type consists of grassland dotted with umbrella thorn bushes that are spaced far apart, and can be seen along the Ntwetwe Pan margin south of Gweta, on the fringes of Lekhubu Island and on Nxai Pan.

### Mixed deciduous woodland

Characterized by large, closely spaced trees, the deciduous woodland consists not only of mopane, but also of a number of other species, most of which are not found elsewhere in the area. Woodland communities can be seen between Nata and Gweta and on the slopes and summit of the Mosu/Kaitshe Escarpment, especially in areas that are rocky areas or that have shallow soils.

The most distinctive tree here is the massive baobab (*Adansonia digitata*). Baobabs are especially common at Kudiakam Pan (near Nxai Pan), on Lekhubu Island and near Gweta (around Planet Baobab Lodge).

Another well-known tree is the marula, which yields smooth, round, edible yellow fruits. These trees are relatively abundant in Nata, Gweta and Sowa Town.

The marula is a most distinctive savanna species.

The bark of the blue-bark corkwood peels off in yellowish or whitish paper strips, revealing a bluish-grey layer underneath.

Floodplain thorn trees thrive near the Nata River Delta.

Grass-like sedges cluster around water pools.

Other woody trees that form part of this vegetation type are the knob thorn and the blue-bark corkwood (*Commiphora caerulea*). The sesame bush (*Sesomothamnus lugardii*), prolific around Mosu, is a soft-stemmed succulent plant; its bark peels off into paper-thin strips to reveal a smooth, rich, brownish or brownish-yellow underbark. It produces large, solitary, white flowers.

### Riverine woodland

This type of woodland, composed of densely spaced tall trees, is most noticeable along the banks of the Nata and Boteti rivers. Here, the deep alluvial soils, a shallow water table and several water pools provide a habitat for several species that occur nowhere else around the pans.

The floodplain thorn (*Vachellia kirkii*) grows along the banks of the Nata River, near the delta. It produces white, ball-shaped flowers and its bark peels to reveal a greenish-yellow underbark that secretes an edible gum. Other species that flourish in this habitat are camel thorn and knob thorn. The buffalo thorn (*Ziziphus mucronata*), with its glossy dark-green leaves and small, reddish-brown berries, is also common. Liana-type plants, twined around the trees as they reach for the canopy, also grow here.

### Aquatic savanna

Several herbaceous water-loving species grow in and around pools in the grassland areas, especially in Nata Bird Sanctuary. The most conspicuous of these is the common reed (*Phragmites australis*), a tall perennial grass with large, cream-brown flower heads, which grows alongside a variety of sedges.

### Disturbed area

Much of the natural vegetation in the vicinity of the villages has been disturbed, or removed, as a result of human activity, with overgrazing and the cutting down of trees for firewood

Wild sage grows profusely near Rakops.

and building being the main culprits. These denuded areas are easily colonized by unwanted invader species such as candlepod acacia and the aromatic wild sage (*Pechuel-loeschea leubnitziae*), the grey-green leaves of which give off a pleasant smell, especially in the early morning.

# Edible plants

There is sufficient evidence to suggest that the Makgidikgadi Pans and environs once sustained small bands of San, the region's original inhabitants. Animals, such as springbok and termites, provided protein; much-needed nutrients were obtained from fruits; and roots and tubers were excellent sources of carbohydrates.

Food from indigenous plants still makes up part of the local diet. Fruits like marula and velvet raisin berries are either consumed fresh or used as a main ingredient in traditional beer. Lesser known is a group of herbaceous climbers whose showy edible fruits and roots are an important source of water for humans and animals alike. These include the jelly melon (*Cucumis metuliferus*), an annual climbing plant that bears oval-shaped orange-red fruits covered with sharp spines, measuring up to 10 millimetres in length, and the gemsbok cucumber (*Acanthosicyos naudinianus*), which is cylindrical in shape and shielded with thick, blunt, conical spines. The fruit pulp and seeds of these species may be eaten raw or roasted in the fire.

The Kalahari cucumber or wild potato (*Cucumis kalahariensis*) grows mainly in areas of deep sand along the Gidikwe Ridge. This perennial creeper is an important source of moisture, starch and minerals. The roots are long and fibrous, containing a white, juicy tissue that may be consumed raw or baked in the fire. The fruit, however, is extremely bitter and is not eaten.

The fruit of the marula tree is a choice food among locals. It is eaten fresh or used in a traditional brew.

The fleshy fruit of the jelly melon may be eaten raw or roasted.

Small herds of springbok congregate around the pans year-round.

# WILDLIFE

To the first-time visitor, the Makgadikgadi Pans may appear monochromatic and featureless, a sandy wasteland covered with grass and scrub. But the range of habitats that occur here guarantees sightings of a wide variety of animals – from gracious antelope and majestic birds to minuscule insects.

## Mammals

The grasslands and bush savanna around the pans draw a vast range of animals throughout the seasons. Drought-adapted mammals, such as steenbok, gemsbok and springbok, are seen year-round, especially in Nata Bird Sanctuary. Further north, towards Nxai Pan, kudu, sable and tsessebe are resident in the mopane woodland.

But it is at the start of the rainy season, in December and January, that the landscape comes alive as vast herds of antelope trek across the countryside to gather around the Makgadikgadi Pans. Drawn by the abundance of fresh green grass and sufficient standing water, zebra and blue wildebeest migrate in their thousands from the Boteti River to the grasslands along the western margins of Ntwetwe Pan.

Each year at the onset of the summer rains, zebra migrate between the Makgadikgadi Pans and the Boteti River.

Once the rains have ended, from May onwards, the animals move westwards, back to the Boteti where they spend the dry winter months around the permanent pools in the river. This is regarded as the second largest migration of wildebeest on the African continent, surpassed only by the annual migration of these grazers in East Africa – between the Serengeti National Park in Tanzania and the Maasai Mara National Reserve in Kenya.

The woodlands around the Boteti River provide refuge for other animals, too, and sightings of grey duiker, kudu, bushbuck, impala and ostrich have been recorded. The trees also provide good cover for chacma baboons and vervet monkeys. One of the permanent pools in the river, Hippo Pool, is home to a population of these semiaquatic mammals. Leopard and even lions may frequent the Boteti area, but sightings are rare.

# Botswana's annual wildebeest migration

Whereas over one million wildebeest take part in the East African migration, the number of animals that constitute the Botswanan migration is much lower. During the 1950s and 1960s, it was estimated that about 60,000 zebra and a similar number of wildebeest made the journey between the Boteti River and Ntwetwe Pan. Since then, large numbers of animals have perished in the droughts that held sway in the area in the 1980s.

A shallow water table supports riverine woodlands along the Boteti River.

More deaths were caused by veterinary fences, put up to control the spread of foot-and-mouth disease. When initially erected, these barriers, which cut across traditional migration routes, prevented the wildebeest from reaching the Boteti. As a result, the animals died in their thousands, their bodies piled up along the fences.

Today, an estimated 35,000 wildebeest and 15,000 zebra make the migration. Spotted hyenas and lions diligently follow the herds.

As winter approaches and the pans dry out, blue wildebeest leave their feeding grounds near Ntwetwe Pan to congregate along the Boteti River.

A ground squirrel uses its tail as protection from the heat.

Elephants occur in large numbers in protected areas, such as Chobe National Park, in northern Botswana, but may migrate southwards during the wet season, venturing as far as Nata and even Sowa Town. North of Nata, along the Kasane road, small pans attract herds of elephant and buffalo during the rains.

Small mammals occur across the grasslands and include yellow mongooses and ground squirrels, which are easily spotted scampering across the tracks. The ground squirrel can withstand the heat by simply fluffing up its thick bushy tail and then using it as a parasol. Another common resident is the springhare, a nocturnal rodent (despite its name) that makes its home in burrows, occupied by individuals or females with their young. Other nocturnal species include the antbear, polecat, genet and scrub hare. Antbears are responsible for most of the larger burrows seen throughout the region.

A species particularly popular with visitors is the suricate, or meerkat, a member of the mongoose family. Regularly seen along the northern shore of Ntwetwe Pan, they live in groups of up to 30 individuals in underground warrens; these have multiple entrances that allow more members to scurry into the den when danger lurks. Despite their small size, meerkats are always hyperactive. One moment they are frantically digging with their front paws for tasty morsels such as beetle larvae, scorpions and millipedes, the next they are standing upright on their hind legs scanning the sky for predators, especially eagles, which can make a meal of a meerkat in seconds. Once the danger has passed, they may resume digging, or start grooming each other, an activity that reinforces bonding within the group and so helps them to survive.

A meerkat looks out for predators.

Antbears live in underground burrows to escape the heat.

# Reading the signs

Even if you do not spot animals in the wild, signs of their whereabouts are all around you. Traces of their presence are found in the markings they leave in the sand and the scat they deposit after feeding.

Tracks most commonly seen in the area include those of springbok and blue wildebeest. Springbok leave behind pointed hoof marks, about 5 centimetres long. In contrast, blue wildebeest are associated with much larger, more oblong-shaped tracks, up to about 10 centimetres long. But the largest feet belong to the elephants; their tracks have an average diameter of 50 centimetres.

Also look out for animal droppings. Springbok produce small, rounded or oval-shaped faecal pellets, up to a centimetre in size. Blue wildebeest deposit similarly shaped droppings, but theirs are larger – about 2 centimetres in size – and clumped together. Zebra have oblong-shaped scat that can measure up to 7 centimetres in length. One or two shallow grooves may also be seen on the surface of their droppings. The owner of the largest scat here is, not surprisingly, the elephant, and its droppings may exceed 20 centimetres in length.

A word of warning, though: avoid handling animal droppings with your bare hands, as they can transmit diseases, worms and parasites.

The tracks of springbok are sharply pointed.

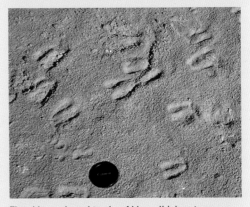
The oblong-shaped tracks of blue wildebeest are easy to spot in soft sand.

A cluster of springbok dung pellets.

A clump of blue wildebeest scat.

Kidney-shaped zebra droppings.

Elephant scat, showing plant fibres.

After the rains, flocks of waterbirds, including lesser and greater flamingoes, descend on Sowa Pan to breed.

### Birdlife

Despite its aridity, the Makgadikgadi Pans region is a birder's paradise, and a staggering 374 bird species have been identified here.

Ntwetwe and Sowa pans, when flooded, are home to over 60 species of waterbird – white-faced ducks, Egyptian geese, red-billed teals, red-billed coots, black-necked grebes, common moorhens, malachite kingfishers, Caspian terns and white pelicans have all been recorded here. Common waders include the pied avocet, African spoonbill, black-winged stilt and common sandpiper. The reedbeds are an ideal habitat for species such as weavers, bishops and African reed warblers.

Perhaps the wading bird that holds the greatest attraction for visitors is the flamingo. Two species occur here: the greater and lesser flamingo. The greater flamingo is a large, slender bird, up to 1.4 metres tall, and has long, pale pink legs, white plumage, and a pink bill with a black tip. The lesser flamingo is smaller, with pinker legs and plumage and a darker bill. In flight, the birds are easily recognized by their beautiful salmon-pink-and-black wings.

Sowa Pan is an important breeding ground for these birds, with flocks of tens of thousands of individuals arriving here from East and southern Africa after good summer rains. In fact, Sowa Pan is one of only a few sites in Africa where the lesser flamingo breeds. The breeding pairs construct small nest mounds made of mud, on top of which a single egg is laid. Then begins the race against time, for it is essential that the young chicks hatch and fledge before the pans dry out. Flamingoes are nomads and, once their young can fly, they move elsewhere, to places where water is more plentiful. A flamingo sanctuary was established in 2010 in the southern part of Sowa Pan in order to protect these breeding sites.

Even when dry, the grasslands support a surprising variety of birds, such as larks, korhaans, guineafowls, sandgrouse and francolins. At dawn, red-billed spurfowl make harsh, cackling sounds as they scamper through the undergrowth. The northern black korhaan,

A red-billed spurfowl forages in the early morning.

with its black head, neck and belly, pink bill and yellow legs, is also a noisy bird, especially in the summer breeding season when it performs spectacular flight displays to attract a potential mate. The male displays by soaring upwards to a height of between 10 and 30 metres before dropping straight down to earth and making harsh 'wak wak' sounds.

Both the world's heaviest flying bird, the kori bustard, and the world's largest bird, the ostrich, are unmistakable residents of the grasslands. With a weight that may approach 20 kilograms, it is not surprising that the kori bustard is reluctant to fly. When it does decide to take to the skies, it usually needs to run some distance before being able to lift itself off the ground. The ostrich is truly adapted to the harsh environment of the Makgadikgadi and can reduce its body heat by panting like a dog. The bird can lower its wings along its flanks to provide shade for its body, and its long legs keep the body well off the scorching ground, allowing for plenty of ventilation.

The secretarybird is easily spotted as it slowly strides across the veld, searching for rats, snakes or lizards. Its name is said to derive from the loose black feathers behind its neck that resemble the quill pens once used by secretaries. Other birds of prey, such as martial and bateleur eagles, roam the skies, while lappet-faced, white-backed and Cape vultures keep a beady eye out for carrion. Greater kestrels, pale chanting goshawks and black kites silently hunt during the day, whereas marsh owls and pearl-spotted owlets swoop down on unsuspecting prey under the cover of darkness. In summer, following the rains, migrant raptors such as the steppe eagle arrive to take advantage of the abundance of food sources, including termites. Other non-resident species that turn up at this time include tawny eagles, Montagu's and pallid harriers.

Throughout the region, stands of trees offer both shelter and food to a range of species.

Ostriches are gregarious, living together in groups.

A pair of kori bustards seek food in the grasslands.

NIGEL J DENNIS/IOA

The long-legged secretarybird is easily spotted in the open veld.

An African spoonbill wades slowly through the water as it forages for food.

The snouted cobra is one of several snake species encountered in the Makgadikgadi area.

The woodlands along the Boteti River are a magnet for African fish eagles, grey go-away-birds, hornbills and Cape glossy starlings. In the palm savanna, to the west of the pans, greater kestrels, palm-nut vultures and African palm swifts nest in the *Hyphaene* trees. The wooded areas of the Makgadikgadi and Nxai Pans National Park are home to lilac-breasted rollers, long-tailed shrikes and magpie shrikes, while larks, finches, warblers and pipits perch on trees near Nxai Pan. Lekhubu Island's baobabs are a majestic setting for the nesting sites of barn owls, lilac-breasted rollers and purple rollers.

Birds that thrive in the Kalahari bush savanna include crowned plovers, black-crowned tchagras, magpies, southern white-crowned shrikes and the secretive crimson-breasted shrike.

### Reptiles

Reptiles are plentiful in Botswana, and several species, ranging from tortoises and rock monitors to snakes and lizards, thrive in the arid expanse of the pans and the grasslands that surround them. The acacia trees are a sought-after habitat for skinks and geckos, whereas agamas and lizards can be encountered in rocky areas, basking in the sun. The Makgadikgadi spiny agama is endemic to the pans, and spotting one could be a highlight

of your visit. This species lives along the edges of the pans, where it buries itself in the sand during the day.

Although seldom encountered, the most common snake species found here include puff adders, black mambas, snouted cobras and African egg-eaters.

Nile crocodiles can be found in the Boteti River. They are resilient and can survive without food for several months. They may even live for several years in holes in the river banks after the water has run dry.

### Invertebrates

Often overlooked, the insects, spiders and scorpions that flourish in and around the Makgadikgadi Pans are fundamental to the intricate web of life in the region.

The termites are the most conspicuous of the insects found here, the dominant species belonging to a subfamily of fungus-growing termites (Macrotermitinae). Their enormous nests are visible for miles across the grasslands. These wingless insects play an important role in decomposing wood and leaf litter and recycling nutrients in the soil. At the same time, they are valuable prey for other species, from spiders to birds and small mammals.

Among the myriad other insects that play a role in the local ecosystem, the dung beetle

PETER & BEVERLY PICKFORD/IOA

A dung beetle rolls animal scat into a ball.

is probably the best known. These efficient cleaners collect animal dung into balls, which they quickly roll away and then bury in the ground. Mating takes place underground, and the female lays her eggs in the dung ball, after which the eggs are fertilized by the male. After the eggs have hatched, the larvae feed on the remaining dung until they have matured into their adult form. As the dung decomposes, nutrients are transferred to the soil, thereby improving soil fertility and stimulating the growth of grazing plants upon which so many animals depend for food.

As its name suggests, the large mopane moth commonly occurs in areas where mopane trees grow. Female moths lay their eggs on the mopane leaves, and the hatchlings – brightly coloured caterpillars equipped with short red or black spines – emerge at the start of the rainy season, in December. In years of good rainfall, a second batch of caterpillars may also hatch at the end of the rains, in April. For the people living around the pans, the worms are a much sought-after delicacy.

On hot summer days, the shrill call of the male cicada, or Christmas beetle, drowns out any other noise. These fly-like insects can be spotted perching on the stems of trees in wooded areas.

Sandy soils are the preferred habitat of antlions. It is here that the larva builds a steep-sided funnel in which to trap unsuspecting prey.

It waits at the bottom of the trap for insects to land on the sides of the funnel; unable to scramble to the top, the prey tumbles down the funnel and into the mouth of an ever-patient antlion.

Closer to the water, dragonflies can be encountered along the shoreline of Sowa Pan. In the same habitat may be seen pond skaters, a wingless, slender-legged species that skims across the surface of the water preying on drowning insects.

The most common arachnids are the orb-web spiders. Their large spiral webs are spun between bushes, directly in the flight path of insects. The spiders usually hang head-down from a strand of silk, ready to catch insects when they land in the web. Their venom is harmless to humans. Not so harmless are the scorpions: the Cape thicktail scorpion and the Kalahari burrower scorpion both live in underground burrows to escape the heat of the day and may lie in wait at the entrance to seize unwary prey. It is not the size of the scorpion that determines how venomous it is, but the size of its tail compared to its pincers. The Cape thicktail scorpion has a thick tail and thin pincers and can cause excruciating pain, and even death. The Kalahari burrower scorpion has a thinner tail and thicker pincers, and a sting from this species will rarely require medical attention.

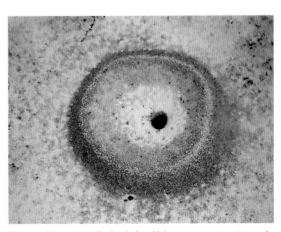

The opening to an antlion's pit, in which unwary prey are trapped.

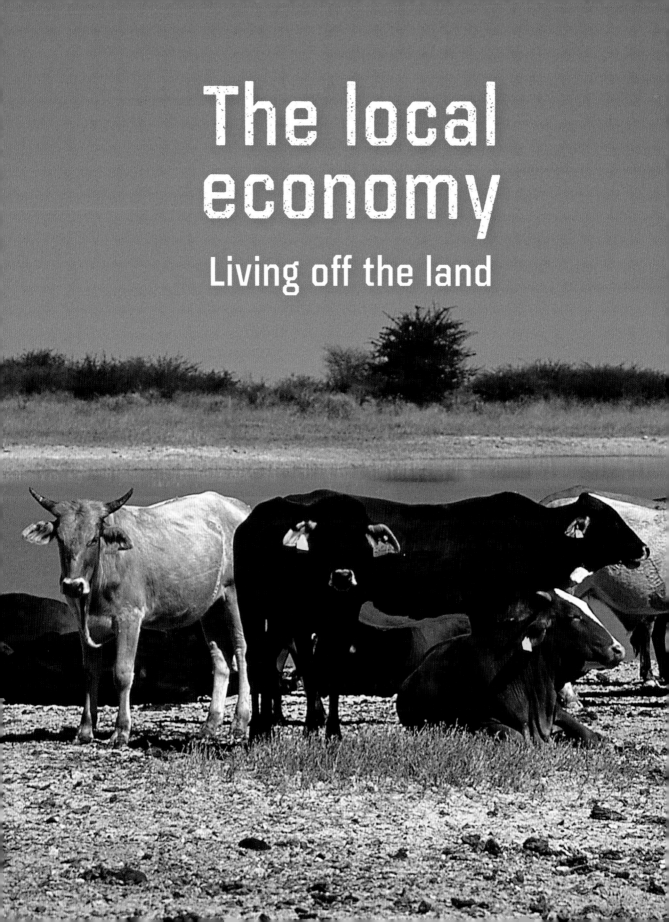

# The local economy

## Living off the land

## CHAPTER 5

While the pans and surrounding areas may appear barren and inhospitable, and the land unproductive, this is not so. The region is rich in natural resources – salts, diamonds, livestock, trees, grasses and insects – that are harnessed to produce wealth, not only for large companies and the government, but for local people as well.

## Salt and soda ash mining

Below the surface of Sowa Pan lies a series of aquifers containing an estimated 8,103 million cubic metres of fossil brines – the source of the salt and soda ash products produced by Botswana Ash (Pty) Ltd.

Located near Sowa Town, Botswana Ash (Botash) began operating in 1991. A partnership between the Botswana government and a South African company, it is the region's largest producer of natural sodium products, with a capacity to process up to 650,000 tonnes of salt and more than 300,000 tonnes of soda ash per annum. It is also one of only two major soda ash producers in Africa; the other is located at Lake Magadi in Kenya.

The underground salt water at Sowa Pan is extracted by means of wells sunk into the saline sands and clays, some of which reach a depth of 38 metres. The salt water solution is rich in sodium, containing 2.75 per cent of soda ash (sodium carbonate) and 13 per cent salt (sodium chloride), making it three times more saline than seawater.

The salt water is pumped from the well field to 14 shallow solar evaporation ponds spanning a surface area of more than 22 square kilometres. Here it may take on a reddish colour due to the presence of halophytic (salt-loving) algae or bacteria; in fact, the pinkish colour of flamingoes living in the area is the result of them ingesting these organisms. To minimize the impact of the well field on the environment, the power cables between the wells and the processing plant were sunk below the surface. This ensures that the flamingoes can fly from their feeding grounds to the north of the plant to their breeding sites to the south free of any obstruction.

Cattle are the backbone of the regional economy and a symbol of personal wealth for many people who live in the vicinity of the Makgadikgadi Pans.

White salt precipitates from reddish-coloured brines in evaporation ponds adjacent to Botash's salt processing plant. Once the salt is harvested (above left), washed and dried, it is ready for export (above right).

After the brine in the ponds has become saturated and the salt has precipitated to produce crystals, the deposits are scraped from the pond floors and transported to the salt plant where they are washed and separated according to size – coarse salt has a particle size of between 0.5 and 10 millimetres, whereas fine salt has a grain size of less than 0.5 millimetres. Once dried, the fine salt is milled to produce table salt, a more refined product. Some salt may also be iodated, making it suitable for domestic use.

Botash's salt products are sold in Botswana and exported to South Africa, Zimbabwe, Zambia, Malawi and the Democratic Republic of the Congo where they are used for domestic purposes and in the chemical industry. Most of the company's soda ash is exported to South Africa where it is used mainly in the manufacture of glass.

## Diamond mining

Botswana is rich in minerals, including diamonds, copper, nickel, coal, uranium, manganese and others. But it is the mining of diamonds that has contributed most to the country's development and the living standards of its people. In recent years, diamonds have

JOHN LEE / DE BEERS

The open-pit Orapa diamond mine is one of the oldest and most productive mining operations in Botswana.

accounted for about 70 per cent of total exports and over 30 per cent of gross domestic product.

It comes as no surprise then that one of the most important economic activities around the Makgadikgadi Pans is the mining of diamonds. Three mines – Orapa, Letlhakane and Damtshaa – operate here, providing employment opportunities for people from the towns of Orapa and Letlhakane, among others.

The Orapa kimberlite pipe, covering an area of 118 hectares, was discovered in 1967. Mining began in 1971 and today Orapa is both the largest conventional open-pit diamond mine and the largest diamond producer by volume in the world. The open pit is now 205 metres deep and measures 1.2 kilometres by 1.8 kilometres.

## Farming

Livestock production is carried out over much of Botswana and beef is the country's only significant agricultural export. In contrast, less than five per cent of the land, mostly near more populated centres in the east, is suitable for successful crop production.

While mining provides some job opportunities for people in the Makgadikgadi area, the main livelihood activity is livestock farming, benefiting about 56 per cent of households. Although some farmers sell small numbers of their cattle to the Botswana Meat Commission's abattoirs in nearby towns, most are subsistence farmers whose animals provide milk, meat, hides and skins for domestic use only. Cattle play a role in crop farming too, serving as draught animals for ploughing fields.

In traditional societies, cattle are associated with social status. Culturally and socially, they represent wealth: in much of Botswana cattle are the most valuable type of livestock and a man's position in his community more often than not depends on the size of his herd. The animals are also used to pay a bride price, or *lobola*. The number of animals paid as *lobola* differs between ethnic groups, but six cows is fairly standard. Other forms of payment include a combination of cows, other livestock, money, and gifts, such as clothes and shoes, given to the parents, uncles and aunts of the bride-to-be.

## Cattle posts

Cattle posts, found in communal grazing areas, are a common sight in Botswana's rural parts. Traditionally, they consist of one or two dwellings for sleeping, kraals for cattle, sheep or goats, and a small granary. The living quarters are rudimentary, made of a variety of materials – mud bricks, or even bricks and mortar, with doors consisting of nothing more than reeds stitched together. The granaries feature pointed conical roofs made of rafters bound together with soil and cow dung. Water may be available from boreholes or collected and stored in water tanks.

Along the Makgadikgadi Pans, cattle posts, usually managed by family groups, have been established outside villages such as Nata and Gweta. Here family members look after the livestock throughout the year. At night, the animals are kept in holding kraals, made from cut thorn bushes or tree branches, to deter predators. In the early morning, the cows are milked before they and the other animals are let out to graze.

Crops are kept in simple mud granaries.

At a cattle post, the day begins early in the morning, with the milking of the family's cows.

Horses are also a common sight in the Makgadikgadi area and are more valuable than livestock. One local man at Mmatshumo mentioned that in his area a cow may fetch a price of P2,500, whereas a horse may easily cost P3,500. The horses are used to round up and herd animals to crushes where they are vaccinated or dipped, or to areas where there is better grazing. For local cattle farmers (Botswana's own 'cowboys'), the horse is one of the most reliable forms of transport; 4x4 vehicles are way beyond their budget and horses survive on grass, a freely available fuel.

The Makgadikgadi region is not suitable for commercial crop farming: poor sandy soils, high summer temperatures, low unreliable rainfall and limited access to markets mean that growing food here is a risky business and crop failure is an all too frequent occurrence. However, subsistence farming is common and farmers survive by practising rain-fed agriculture, using very few inputs, and carrying out traditional methods of farming. They grow traditional varieties of crops, including sorghum, maize, millet, beans and watermelon – all mainly for domestic use. Despite the many challenges these farmers face, 72 per cent of households around the pans benefit from crop farming.

# Veld products

Veld products – natural resources obtained by people from animals and plants found in the veld – are vital to the livelihoods of many people living around the pans. Products such as grass, mopane worms, palm leaves and firewood are harvested and processed into a range of items that are used domestically and made available for sale.

### Harvesting grass

The pan fringes are covered in deep sand, an ideal habitat for broom love grass, *Eragrostis pallens*, which has hard stems that are suitable for making brooms. Other grasses include broad-leaved turpentine grass (*Cymbopogon excavatus*) and common thatching grass (*Hyparrhenia hirta*) – both of which grow along the verges of roads in the region.

Grass harvesting is an inexpensive activity, usually done with simple tools such as scythes, and there are no seeds, fertilizers, pesticides or heavy machinery to buy. The only cost is labour, provided by the harvesters themselves, usually middle-aged women who may be assisted by close family members.

Grass is harvested mainly by women, using simple tools such as scythes (top). Neatly bundled, the harvested grass is sold on the side of the road to Kasane, north of Nata (above).

Harvesting of grasses is allowed only between 15 July and 20 October. Since the summer rains usually end by April, the grasses would have dried out, hardened and dispersed their seeds by July. After October, harvesting is not permitted since the grasses are actively growing, flowering and producing seed.

During harvest time, the grass cutters move from their villages to temporary shelters situated along the Kasane road north of Nata. The harvested grass is trimmed and tied into bundles – the smaller ones to make traditional brooms and the larger ones to be used for thatching. Although the harvesters use some of the grass to thatch their own rondavels, they sell the surplus to local villagers or passers-by. The owners of lodges and guest houses make up another group of buyers, and the Kasane road becomes a hive of activity when their trucks descend on the grass cutters' settlement to load up on thatching grass.

Hundreds, or even thousands, of pula may change hands during harvesting season. In 2016/17, the value of grass harvested by 880 Gweta households came to about P9 million.

### Baskets

Some women collect the young leaves of the real fan palm (*Hyphaene petersiana*) throughout the year to produce baskets largely for domestic use. In 2016/17, it was estimated that this activity brought in P340,000 to households in Gweta.

### Mopane worms

High in protein and fat, the caterpillar of the emperor moth (*Imbrasia belina*) has long been a source of food for people throughout northern Botswana. It is no different around the pans, where the caterpillars, known as mopane worms, or *phane*, are harvested for domestic consumption and for commercial sale.

The caterpillars feed almost exclusively on the leaves of the mopane tree (*Colophospermum*

Dried mopane worms are a staple food in many villages.

*mopane*), one of the most recognizable plants in southern Africa. The worms are usually harvested twice a year: in April/May and December/January. They may be eaten fresh or cooked and dried in the sun. The dehydrated mopane worms may be eaten as a snack or cooked with vegetables. They can be kept for up to a year, mostly for consumption in lean times.

Mopane worms are sold locally in villages, along main roads, or to traders. On average, households earn around P3,000 per year from the sale of these worms.

### Firewood

Firewood is used for cooking by almost 80 per cent of households, even though its importance is slowly decreasing due to an increased use of paraffin and gas. Preferred species include mopane, leadwood (*Combretum imberbe*) and knob thorn (*Senegalia nigrescens*). It is estimated that some 950,000 headloads of wood are collected annually around the pans, and its value to households in Gweta in 2016/17 was about P3.6 million. The continued harvesting of firewood is a matter of concern, with some species being heavily depleted.

## Traditional beer and wine

Another activity carried out by the locals is making alcoholic drinks: marula beer, palm wine and *khadi*.

Locals brew beer from fermented marula berries (above) and distil wine using sap collected from palm trees (right).

## Marula beer

Marula trees (*Sclerocarya birrea*) grow mainly between Nata and Gweta. The marula, a medium-sized tree, typically grows to about 15 metres in height. It is highly valued for its nutritional fruit – a large, hard seed enclosed by a greyish, juicy pulp that contains four times as much vitamin C as an orange. Harvested between February and April, the ripened fruits are readily eaten fresh, but most are used in the brewing of beer.

The beer is usually made by women at their homes, especially in the larger villages of Nata and Gweta. Once ripened, the fruits are peeled and placed in large pots of water for a few days to allow fermentation to take place. Marula beer, known locally as *chikoto*, has an eight per cent alcohol content, giving this local brew a powerful kick! While some of the beer is consumed domestically, most of it is sold. The average annual value of beer brewing in 2016/17 was P2,665 per household.

## Palm wine

The real fan palm, known locally as *mokolwane*, is common in Nata and in areas to the west of Gweta. Here, a white sap is harvested from the trees. The sap may be mixed with porridge, as a substitute for milk, but is more commonly used to make palm wine, a relatively sweet drink that tastes like good quality ginger beer. For

those hooked on stronger stuff, the palm wine may be further distilled into a highly potent spirit – about 20 litres of wine produces 2 litres of firewater. Most wine is sold to local villagers.

To collect the sap, the stem is cut just above ground level and the tip trimmed with a sharp knife to initiate a flow. The substance then drips into a container by means of a funnel attached to the stem. A single tree may yield up to 70 litres of sap.

## Khadi

The velvet raisin (*Grewia flava*) is a small bush that produces yellow flowers and small, reddish-brown berry-like fruits that are harvested by women in late summer. Although the fruits are eaten fresh, they may also be mixed with water and sugar to make a traditional brew known as *khadi*. Some brewers add soil from termite mounds to quicken fermentation.

# Towns
# and villages
## From Gweta to Khumaga

## CHAPTER 6

The Makgadikgadi area is more than just salt pans, wildlife, flamingoes and savanna. People live here, and their rich culture and traditions are on display everywhere – from Gweta and Nata, the largest of the settlements along the northern rim of the pans, to Mopipi and Khumaga, some of the smallest villages along the southern and western margins of the pans.

Visitors may regard these places as no more than pit stops on the long road to Maun, Moremi Game Reserve, the Okavango Delta or the Chobe National Park. But it is worth lingering in these towns and villages, taking time to walk their dusty streets, admiring the beautiful traditional homes and partaking of the local cuisine. Each place also serves as a launch pad for exploring the pans and pursuing any number of activities available for travellers and adventurers.

Most of the towns and villages along the way cater for travellers and offer accommodation facilities and basic goods and services.

## GWETA

Located in the shade of large marula (*Sclerocarya birrea*) trees, Gweta is a small village halfway between Francistown and Maun and some 100 kilometres west of Nata. Several tracks lead from here to Ntwetwe Pan and the Makgadikgadi and Nxai Pans National Park.

The village provides a few basic facilities, including a general dealer, a police station and a government primary hospital. A small vehicle- and puncture-repair shop is open during working hours from Monday to Friday. Although the village has a filling station, fuel is not always available, and travellers are advised to rather fill up in Nata or Maun.

Like Nata, Gweta's 4,000 residents include the Bakalanga (who are related to the Shona of Zimbabwe), the Basarwa (San) and the Bamangwato, the latter occupying much of the area between Mahalapye in the south and the Makgadikgadi Pans in the north.

A typical rural family dwelling in the region consists of a few huts for sleeping and a courtyard that serves as the kitchen and sitting room.

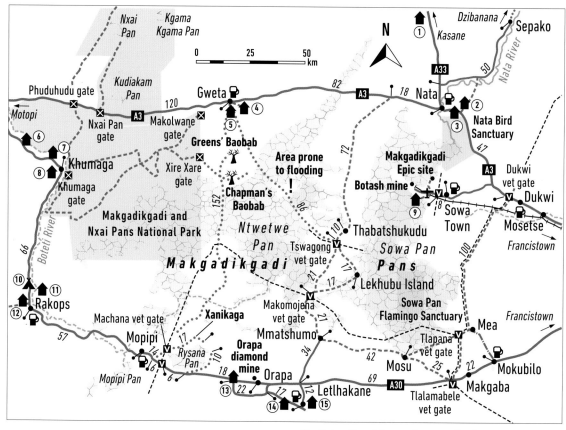

The Makgadikgadi Pans and surrounding towns.

## LODGES AND CAMPS

1. Elephant Sands Bush Lodge & Campsite
2. Nata Lodge
3. Pelican Lodge and Camping
4. Planet Baobab
5. Gweta Lodge
6. Meno a Kwena Camp
7. Leroo La Tau
8. Boteti River Camp
9. Makgadikgadi Lodge
10. Matsaudi Camp Site
11. Rakops River Lodge
12. Xere Motel
13. Makumutu Lodge and Campsite
14. Tuuthebe Lodge and Campsite
15. Mikelele Motel

## KEY

- ● Town/village
- ▲ Camp site
- ⬆ Lodge
- ⛽ Filling station
- ✕ Entrance gate
- Ⓥ Vet gate
- ⌐10⌐ Distance in kilometres
- —— Main/tarred road
- —·—· Track (any vehicle)
- - - - Track (2x4 pickup truck/4x4)
- ···· Track (4X4 only)
- ┼┼┼ Railway
- ---- Vet fence
- —— River
- — — Seasonal river
- ⟆ Pan

The area around Gweta and the pans has a long history of human settlement. Stone tools found at different locations in the region point to intermittent settlement during the Middle and Later Stone Ages by hunter-gatherers, the ancestors of the modern-day San. Most of the artefacts found in the area and around Ntwetwe Pan are made from black silcrete, taken from the pan's surface. Handaxes – stone tools with a sharpened end and a rounded base – were the first tools to be made by early humans, and they may have been used to slaughter animals, dig for tubers, chop wood and loosen tree bark. Other tools included cleavers for cutting up large pieces of meat; scrapers to remove flesh from hides; and arrowheads and spearheads, which were attached to wooden shafts.

# Giants of the savanna

Thriving in clusters or growing singly, the baobabs (*Adansonia digitata*) in the vicinity of Gweta are prominent features in the landscape, and the best-known specimens, Greens' Baobab and Chapman's Baobab, occur south of the village.

Greens' Baobab, close to the eastern boundary of the Makgadikgadi and Nxai Pan National Park, got its name from Frederick and Charles Green who once camped under the tree on their way to Matabeleland in Zimbabwe. The brothers, both traders and explorers, left their mark by carving the words 'Green's Expedition 1858–1859' into the bark of the tree.

The massive Chapman's Baobab lies near the northern shoreline of Ntwetwe Pan. This giant, estimated to be nearly 3,000 years old, was blown over by strong winds in January 2017. Its presence was first recorded in 1861 by James Chapman, a South African trader and explorer who accompanied Thomas Baines to the region. The tree has a circumference of more than 25 metres and boasts seven trunks – the source of its local nickname 'Seven Sisters'. It was also known as the Post Office Tree, as early explorers, such as David Livingstone and Frederick Selous, are said to have left messages for each other in a large hole, about 2 metres from the ground, in a trunk of the tree.

Once signposts for early explorers, traders and missionaries who passed through this area, these trees are now national monuments.

Chapman's Baobab grows amid grasses on Ntwetwe Pan. The gap in a trunk of the tree (above right) once served as a repository for messages left by early explorers.

Before 1938, Gweta's schoolchildren were taught under this marula tree.

The first written records of human presence at modern-day Gweta date to the 1920s, when the San, attracted by a good supply of water and abundant game, began to cluster around the water holes that filled up after the rains. By 1923, other groups, including the Kalanga, joined them. The Kalanga put down roots at a water hole surrounded by baobabs, called Gozoba, a San name

## Traditional architecture in Gweta and Nata

To many visitors a traditional African hut is little more than mud walls and a roof of thatch. But there is much more to these ubiquitous buildings – many of which are surprisingly elaborate and eye-catching.

Most huts are circular and consist of only one room. Making the walls of the hut is women's work. Bricks are made of a mixture of dried cow dung, soil from termite mounds and water. Once the wall is up, it is then plastered. Every year, usually in spring, women replaster their huts since the walls are easily damaged by rain.

Constructing the conical-shaped roof is men's work. Vertical poles are erected at intervals around the perimeter of the hut to support the roof. A network of beams, rafters and purlins, tied together with strips of tree bark or wire, is then constructed on top of the poles. Finally, the roof is thatched, a job executed by the women. Loose grass is laid on top of the roof structure and then fixed to the rafters and beams by strips of tree bark.

In most huts, the roof usually extends beyond the outer wall to form a cover for the raised mud platform that encircles the base of the dwelling. This 'veranda' provides much-needed shade and is a favourite place for the elders to pass the time of day chatting.

Bricks are made from cow manure, soil and water.

A sturdy tree trunk is used to support the thatched roof.

that describes the skinning of animals after a hunt. The village was formally established in 1930 by the then British colonial government, which was also responsible for building the Gweta Primary School in 1938 – the first classes were taught in the shade of a large marula tree, which is still standing today.

Due to the presence of cattle, wildlife sightings are not very common. One species that can be seen, though, is the meerkat, and clans of 20 or more meerkats can be observed along the northern margin of Ntwetwe Pan. These animals are active during the day, getting going shortly after sunrise when they can be seen huddling close together. According to local guides, the meerkats have become rather tame, and any human sitting down on the ground is an open invitation for one of these creatures to climb onto them.

Another reason for the canopy is to stop rainwater from dripping close to the base of the hut wall, as this may weaken the wall and eventually lead to the collapse of the hut.

Most huts are fronted by an open courtyard – a mud floor, sometimes patterned, surrounded by a low wall. The wall is plastered in a similar way to the hut wall and the top section is sometimes finished off with a wavy or crenellated edge.

A corner of the courtyard serves as an open-air kitchen. Taking centre stage is the fireplace, or hearth, usually just a shallow basin in the floor where the family meal will be cooked in three-legged cast-iron pots. The hearth plays an important role in local culture and is a place of much social activity. Not only is it a gathering place for family members and visitors, it is also where arrangements for social events, such as weddings and funerals, are made.

Courtyard floors are typically adorned with patterns.

A scalloped edge enhances this freshly replastered wall.

The evening meal is prepared in the open courtyard.

Planet Baobab is famous for its quirky design (above and right).

## Places to stay

### Planet Baobab

Situated about 95 kilometres west of Nata, along the Nata–Maun road, and 5 kilometres before the turnoff to Gweta, Planet Baobab is a welcome, if quirky, oasis in the vastness of the Kalahari. The colourful lodgings, nestled in the shade of massive baobabs, are inspired by the traditional Kalanga-style homes scattered across the northern Botswana landscape. The exterior walls of the thatched rondavels are adorned with vibrant patterned murals, while inside, the huts, all with en-suite bathrooms, are light and bright, with a touch of colour. There is also a camp site with generously sized stands, thatched shelters for shade, and ablution facilities

The lodge's large thatched bar is the social heart of the place. Featuring stools and chairs covered with Nguni cattle hides, walls festooned with old black-and-white photographs and maps, and a large chandelier, fashioned from recycled beer bottles, the funky bar is an obligatory spot for sundowners.

### Gweta Lodge

Originally a trading store stood on the site where Gweta Lodge is today. It was established in 1965, but changed hands several times,

serving variously as a hardware store and a hunter's camp, before its present owner turned it into a haven for travellers in 2004.

Situated in Gweta village itself, the lodge offers comfortable accommodation in luxury en-suite rooms, equipped with air conditioning or ceiling fans and mosquito nets. Accommodation is also available in thatched rondavels, and a camp site serves those who prefer sleeping in their own tent. Additional facilities include a restaurant offering breakfast, lunch and supper, and a bar adjacent to the swimming pool.

### Chaixara Backpackers

Situated 3 kilometres outside Gweta, Chaixara Backpackers is next to a permanent water hole. Chaixara, meaning 'water source' in Sesarwa (the language of the Basarwa), consists of a dormitory and a camp site. Only solar power is used here, and fresh water is extracted from a nearby water hole. Other amenities include a swimming pool and a bar with a pool table. The road to the camp is suitable for saloon cars.

# NATA

Nata is strategically located along the highway between Francistown and Maun. From Nata, another road leads to Kasane and the Chobe National Park, making it an ideal stopover en route to the rugged north. But its reputation as a gateway to other destinations obscures the attractions of the village itself. Located close to the northern rim of Sowa Pan, it is an ideal springboard for exploring the great salt pans of the Makgadikgadi, the spectacular birdlife of Nata Bird Sanctuary (see Chapter 9) at the northeastern end of Sowa Pan, and the cultural traditions of the people living around the pans.

The village is home to more than 5,000 people, made up of the Kalanga, the Setswana-speaking Bangwato and the Basarwa. This is cattle-farming country, and many of the local inhabitants keep livestock of some kind at small settlements, or cattle posts, away from the village.

There is a range of basic facilities for travellers in the village centre, including filling stations, vehicle repair garages, accommodation, restaurants, general dealers, a supermarket, a butchery, a police station, a bank, and private and government clinics.

# Places to stay

There are several places to stay in Nata village, ranging from the unfussy to the semi-luxurious, with most featuring en-suite rooms with showers or baths, air conditioning and TV. Offering good value for money, these establishments include Northgate Lodge, Maya Lodge, Nata Guest Inn and Gomwe Guest Inn. Two other establishments – Nata Lodge and Pelican Lodge and Camping – lie outside the village along the Francistown road. Both are popular stopovers for visitors who wish to spend a few days in the region. Further afield are Elephant Sands Bush Lodge & Campsite and Dzibanana Lodge and Camping.

## Nata Lodge

Nine kilometres from Nata and nestled among tall palm trees is Nata Lodge, a collection of thatched chalets, safari tents and a camp site. Facilities such as a restaurant, bar, TV lounge, swimming pool, conference centre, curio shop and internet connectivity make for a comfortable stay. Take care when driving in the camp site though; some sections of the track are covered with deep, loose sand and may only be accessible to 4x4 vehicles.

UNDER ONE BOTSWANA SKY

The thatched bar and open-air dining area at Nata Lodge is an ideal place to relax after a long day out on the pans.

The thatch-roofed reception office at Pelican Lodge.

## Pelican Lodge and Camping

Five kilometres east of Nata is Pelican Lodge and Camping, offering a selection of thatched bungalows and chalets, as well as a camping site with ablution facilities.

A highlight of your stay here will be the array of traditional dishes (known by both their English and Setswana names) served at the lodge's Boma Restaurant. Start with sorghum beer, followed by hors d'oeuvres such as mopane worms (*phane*), peanuts in their shells (*manoko*), Bambara groundnuts (*ditloo*), snot apple fruit (*morojwa*) and water lily stems (*tswii*). The main course is a smorgasbord of different dishes: maize meal porridge (*paletshe*), sorghum porridge (*mabele*), game stew, wild spinach (*merogo ya Setswana*) and boiled marrow (*marotse*) are regular menu items. Soft sorghum porridge (*motogo*) is served at breakfast.

## Elephant Sands Bush Lodge & Campsite

Elephant Sands, a 16,000-hectare private conservancy, lies 52 kilometres north of Nata on the road to Kasane. Originally a small resort, mainly for family and friends, the place has grown into a destination of international renown. Although the first two bungalows built here in 2002 are still in use, the establishment has matured into a welcoming wilderness retreat, styled to guarantee an authentic bush experience. Lodgings include safari tents and chalets, as well as a camp site, all designed to blend in with the natural environment.

But the main drawcard here is the water hole, a gathering place for hundreds of elephants that come here to quench their thirst and enjoy the occasional mud bath. Visitors can watch them frolic in style, sundowners in hand as the sun sets across the savanna.

Although there is a higher concentration of elephants in the reserve during the dry season, these gargantuan animals are usually present year-round – along with other wild animals such as buffalo, steenbok, impala, kudu, zebra, jackal, giraffe and lion. There may be also good sightings of African wild dog.

Bush birds commonly seen include magpie shrikes, southern white-crowned shrikes, black-crowned tchagras, and two of the sandveld's most distinctive birds: the Kalahari scrub robin and the crimson-breasted shrike. A common sight is the red-billed spurfowl, which can be spotted pecking at the ground, searching for seeds and small invertebrates. The skies are the domain of raptors such as tawny and bateleur eagles.

Wild animals such as elephants (top) and African wild dogs (above) can be seen at Elephant Sands Bush Lodge & Campsite.

# Saving the elephants

Elephant Sands is home to the Water for Elephants Trust, a non-profit organization that installs and maintains boreholes in former hunting areas in eastern Botswana.

The boreholes are intended to serve as a lifeline for an increasing number of elephants and other species who have to travel vast distances in search of drinking water during the dry season. For a time, the water hole at Elephant Sands, fed by a borehole, represented the only source of drinking water for hundreds of elephants in the region. The crowded conditions around the water source inevitably led to fractious behaviour among the thirsty behemoths.

A water hole at Elephant Sands Lodge provides much-needed relief for thirsty elephants.

By developing more boreholes over a much larger territory, it is hoped not only to relieve the bottleneck at Elephant Sands, but also to create a much larger expanse across which the elephants can range when searching for surface water and food resources. It is estimated that each new borehole will provide water for about 800 elephants.

## Dzibanana Lodge and Camping

A bit further afield – some 70 kilometres northeast of Nata and 12 kilometres from Sepako, adjacent to the Zimbabwe border – is Dzibanana Lodge, built around large permanent pools that have formed in the Nata River. Around the pool margins are leadwood (*Combretum imberbe*) and mopane (*Colophospermum mopane*) trees. From here,

The chalets at Dzibanana Lodge are all built on stilts.

the river flows south on its way to Sowa Pan through magnificent mopane woodlands.

The pools are a magnet for wildlife: buffalo, elephant, kudu, bushbuck, blue wildebeest, hartebeest, impala, hyena, jackal and lion are some of the species that can be seen here. Several bush bird species occur in the woodlands, and it is not unusual to spot fork-tailed drongos, bushshrikes, Retz's helmetshrikes and glossy starlings flitting from tree to tree. In the pools, jacanas may be seen striding across floating lily leaves, while African openbills wade in shallow water along the margins. Watch out for African fish eagles perching at the top of large mopane or knob thorn trees.

This tranquil scene is the setting for 12 fully equipped thatched chalets, all of which are en suite with showers. There is a basic camp site with a communal ablution block. The restaurant offers breakfast, lunch and dinner daily, and all meals must be prebooked. A stunning bar overlooks two large river pools.

Botash Conservation Park, a private wildlife sanctuary abutting Sowa Pan, is home to a multitude of species, including flamingoes.

BOTSWANA ASH (PTY) LTD

## SOWA TOWN

Approximately 137 kilometres along the Francistown–Nata road, a turnoff leads westwards to Sowa Town, some 20 kilometres away. It is a relatively new settlement, and many of the approximately 4,000 residents work in the nearby Botash salt mine.

Sowa Town offers visitors a few basic facilities, including a filling station, a small supermarket, private and government clinics and a police station. There are no banks or overnight facilities.

The landscape here is covered in mopane scrub, but gives way to grassland dotted with black thorn (*Senegalia mellifera*) and velvet raisin (*Grewia flava*) bushes along Sowa Pan. Large marula trees grow in the village itself.

Wildlife is generally sparse, although elephant commonly feed among the mopane scrub in the area between the Francistown–Nata road and Sowa Town. They are known to strip the bark off mopane bushes and have even knocked down taller mopane trees. Well-worn elephant trails crisscross the terrain and give a clue as to the movement of these gargantuan mammals, and travellers who are lucky enough may observe them taking a mud bath in hollows along the road to Sowa Town in the late afternoon.

Elephant numbers have increased significantly in recent years, resulting in large migrations from their original range to areas previously not inhabited by them. Many of these mammals seen around Sowa Town have moved southwards from their traditional haven in Chobe National Park.

The Botash Conservation Park, a sanctuary located along a section of Sowa Pan near the Botash plant, is home to several wildlife species, some of which have been reintroduced into the area from other parts of Botswana and from South Africa. Wild animals such as hyena, jackal, blue wildebeest, ostrich, eland, zebra, impala and springbok can be spotted in the grasslands adjacent to the road between Sowa Town and the Botash plant. In 2017 the park was given a donation of four rhinoceros, a generous gift from the Khama Rhino Sanctuary near Serowe. Plans are afoot to develop a camp site and other facilities for visitors. Botash also plans to add more game animals to the park and extend its boundaries further north to Nata Bird Sanctuary.

## Places to stay

### Makgadikgadi Lodge

Approximately 17 kilometres west of Sowa Town, Makgadikgadi Lodge offers visitors a choice between thatched chalets and budget rooms, all equipped with showers, toilets and air conditioning. There is also a basic camp site, and dome tents with beds, mattresses and bedding can be hired.

# Things to do

## Gweta, Nata and Sowa Town

### Cultural tours

A cultural tour of a village – a mix of modern and traditional homes – provides a fascinating insight into the life, culture and traditions of the local inhabitants.

GWETA: Both Gweta Lodge and Planet Baobab offer guided walks in this village. Depending on which establishment's excursion you choose to join, you'll visit the local primary school, a traditional healer, the home of a local traditional basket weaver, or a cattle post. A traditional lunch is included in Planet Baobab's tour.

NATA: Nata, Pelican and Northgate lodges offer cultural tours of this local village; these typically include a visit to the *kgotla* (a customary court or public meeting place), a local school, a traditional compound (residential areas usually housing family groups) and the Nata River.

Pelican Lodge also organizes cultural tours to the neighbouring village of Manxotae, which lies 25 kilometres northeast of Nata. These tours include a traditional lunch, making them very popular with visitors.

### Bush walks

GWETA: Knowledgeable guides from both Planet Baobab and Gweta Lodge will share fascinating facts about the ecology and history of the baobab 'forest' near Gweta. Choose between a leisurely amble among these trees or join a late-afternoon walk that concludes with sundowners.

NATA: Pelican Lodge runs short bush walks in the Nata area. Further afield, at Elephant Sands, professional guides take visitors on informative hikes through the bush, where they learn about the vegetation and the many uses of local plants, wildlife, and how to identify animal tracks.

### Trips to Ntwetwe Pan

GWETA: Both Gweta Lodge and Planet Baobab organize half-day, full-day and overnight trips to Ntwetwe Pan. These are packed with activities: visiting Greens' and Chapman's baobabs, observing resident meerkats along the margin of the pan, taking a ride on a quad bike, and viewing Stone Age tools are all on a list of things to tick off. Lunches and cold beverages are provided as part of the day excursions.

The overnight trips are highly recommended. After supper, usually a delicious braai, guests can enjoy the solitude of the pan before settling down to sleep in bedrolls under a star-studded sky.

### Off-road driving

GWETA: There are several tracks to explore, most of which lead to Ntwetwe Pan, some 40 kilometres south from Gweta. Driving on Ntwetwe Pan is not recommended, especially if conditions are wet.

NATA: Guests at Elephant Sands can explore the conservancy, using their own 4x4 vehicles.

Clans of 20 or more meerkats can be observed along the margin of Ntwetwe Pan.

## Game drives

**NATA:** The organized guided game drive at Elephant Sands is highly recommended. Early-morning and late-afternoon drives in the lodge's conservancy or the nearby CT/5 wildlife management area are an opportunity to survey the landscape from the comfort of an open-sided vehicle. Sightings of elephants are guaranteed and there is a good chance of also spotting buffaloes, giraffes, African wild dogs, hyenas, steenbok and lions.

Pelican Lodge and Northgate Lodge also organize trips to the CT/5 wildlife management area north of Nata.

## Skydiving

**SOWA TOWN:** Some call it the Makgadikgadi Epic Skydiving Boogie and Symposium; others know it simply as the Makgadikgadi Epic. Launched in 2014, this annual four-day extravaganza of activities, hosted by the Botswana Tourism Organisation in association with Skydive Botswana and the Nata Conservation Trust, is now an international event, drawing adrenalin junkies and their families from countries around the globe. The Epic is held along the shore of Sowa Pan during the President's Day long weekend, usually the second weekend in July. It is open to both expert skydivers and novices, who, for a fee, are welcome to book a tandem jump with an experienced instructor. Other fun-filled activities on the programme are horse riding, quad biking and go-carting. Water activities include jet-skiing or taking a trip on a hovercraft. Helicopter flips are also on offer.

Registration for the event opens several months in advance and the fee includes accommodation in dome tents (equipped with beds, mattresses and bedding) and gourmet-style meals. Camping may also be possible in Sowa Town at a temporary camp site.

The annual Makgadikgadi Epic draws skydivers from near and far to Sowa Town for an adrenalin-filled long weekend (above). For the more cautious adventurer, a trip in a hovercraft across the placid waters of Sowa Pan may be more appealing (top).

The Race for Rhinos, involving single-engined aircrafts (above), raises money to protect the rhino (top), an endangered species.

### Flying for charity
SOWA TOWN: Now in its fourth year, the popular Race for Rhinos – an air race for single-engined aircraft – is a two-day event held annually in July near Sowa Town. The race is organized by the Botswana Tourism Organisation and the Matsieng Flying Club. In 2018, 116 aircraft took part, setting a new record for the highest number of single-engined flying machines simultaneously taking part in a single race. Held in aid of rhino conservation, the air race attracts competitors from all corners of the globe, including southern Africa, the Americas, Australia, the United Kingdom, Switzerland, Italy and Hong Kong. An added thrill is a small-scale air show featuring aerobatic flight displays.

### Golf
SOWA TOWN: The Makgadikgadi Country Club has an 18-hole golf course set amid the dry sands of Sowa Town. With the fairways and 'greens' giving the appearance of a massive bunker, a round here will certainly challenge your putting skills.

# LETLHAKANE
Letlhakane is the gateway to the southern shoreline of the Makgadikgadi Pans. It may be reached from the south along the A4 road from Palapye and Serowe.

Letlhakane started out as a small traditional village in 1939, but saw a significant increase in the population following the establishment of several diamond mines in the region in the 1970s. Today, the town serves the nearby Debswana-owned Letlhakane diamond mine. It is well resourced, with several schools, a hospital and clinics, service stations, banks and supermarkets.

## Places to stay
### Mikelele Motel
Located in Letlhakane, the Mikelele Motel is a comfortable establishment, offering affordable accommodation in either en-suite rooms or bungalows. Breakfasts, lunches and dinners are included and there is a bar area.

### Makumutu Lodge and Campsite
Makumutu Lodge and Campsite is located at the Orapa turnoff, some 39 kilometres west of Letlhakane along the Maun road. Accommodation is available in large en-suite safari tents and dome tents, while campers have a pick of six spacious stands.

The bar at Makumutu Lodge and Campsite.

Situated on the outskirts of Orapa on rehabilitated land, the Orapa Game Park protects a wide variety of mammals, including impala.

## Tuuthebe Lodge and Campsite

Offering both lodge and camping facilities, Tuuthebe is 5 kilometres west of Letlhakane, along the road to Maun. The approach to the lodge leads through an orchard beyond which are several spacious self-catering chalets, each featuring a kitchen (with a mini fridge, microwave and hotplate), sitting room, bedroom and en-suite bathroom. They are also well equipped, with air conditioning, a TV and a braai stand outside at the back.

There is a very attractive camp site with shade trees, lawns and a series of small lakes. Seven stands are available; each one has a wooden table and benches, a braai stand, dish-washing facilities, an electric light and power points. Ablutions are communal.

Tuuthebe Lodge and Campsite features a string of small lakes.

For those travellers not equipped with the necessary camping gear, dome tents can be rented. These come with beds, mattresses, bedding and towels.

## ORAPA

A small modern town, Orapa serves one of the world's most productive diamond mines. Orapa diamond mine, approximately 240 kilometres from Francistown, exploits two separate kimberlite pipes, formed approximately 93 million years ago. Although Orapa has a wide range of facilities, visitors can only enter the town if they have obtained an entry permit from the Debswana mining office in Orapa.

The Orapa Game Park lies on the outskirts of the town. It was established in 1985 on land that had been badly degraded by cattle grazing and recreational use. Almost 49,000 hectares in extent, the fenced park conserves a variety of animals, including springbok, kudu, blue wildebeest, eland, waterbuck and giraffe. It also contributes to the conservation of birdlife and conducts research into threatened species occurring in the park, such as the lappet-faced vulture. Since it lies within the Orapa town boundary, a permit is required to visit the game park.

# The Boteti River – Lifeline from the Okavango

On the western side of the Makgadikgadi Pans, the Boteti River cuts a green swathe through the sandy wastes of the sun-baked Kalahari wilderness. It is indeed an oasis, and its life-giving waters attract large herds of wild animals, especially during the dry season.

The Boteti River is a verdant oasis during the wet season.

The Boteti has its source in the Okavango Delta, which was created when the Botswana Rift Valley formed approximately 10,000 years ago (see Chapter 2). An overflow of water from this vast inland delta gave birth to a new river, the Thamalakane, which today flows southwestwards through Maun towards Lake Ngami. Some 20 kilometres southwest of where Maun is today, some of the Thamalakane's waters escaped through a gap, or weakness, in the Thamalakane fault, to produce the Boteti. This new river then cleaved its own course through the landscape to reach the southwest corner of Ntwetwe Pan.

The floodplain of the Boteti River was formed by the deposition of alluvial materials – such as greyish-black loams and clays – during times of flooding when the river burst its banks and inundated large areas. The floodplain is covered with areas of treeless grassland and is visible between Mopipi and Khumaga. Other common floodplain features such as meanders, oxbow lakes and braided channels may still be seen in the area in times of good rains.

In modern times the river has been at the mercy of cycles consisting of wet and dry phases. During wet years, the river may flow as far as Rakops, and may occasionally reach Ntwetwe Pan. During long dry phases, bushes and trees may take root along the waterless riverbed, only to die when the river starts flowing again. Trees that have died as a result of being flooded in this manner may be seen in the riverbed at Rakops River Lodge.

The waterway does not ever completely dry up; deep pools occur, even in dry years. The river did not flow for many years, but the return of water during a new wet phase that began in 2010 has attracted plenty of wildlife.

The river banks are lined with calcrete cliffs and beautiful camel thorn (*Vachellia erioloba*) woodlands, which provide ample shade for the lodges and camp sites located along the course of the river between Mopipi and Maun.

Some trees that germinate and grow in the Boteti's dry riverbed may actually die off when the river fills with water again. Some dead specimens can be seen along the river at Rakops River Lodge.

## MOPIPI

The small village of Mopipi, between Orapa and Rakops, lies on a low ridge amid an expanse of grasslands and black thorn bushes. From the village, there are good views of Mopipi Pan. Now dry, the large salt pan once functioned as a reservoir in which water pumped from the nearby Boteti River was stored before being channelled to the Orapa diamond mine.

Immediately west of Mopipi, the main road crosses a number of low calcrete ridges.

Facilities in Mopipi include two filling stations, one of which has a convenience store and sells takeaways, a few general dealers and a puncture-repair service.

There are several camping spots along Mopipi Pan, reached by taking any number of tracks leading from the main road in the village to the pan. Out of respect for the local residents, it is best not to camp too close to the village.

## RAKOPS

A quaint village of huts and bungalows scattered over a wide area, Rakops is the largest settlement along the Boteti River. Situated on the road to Maun, it is also a gateway to the Central Kalahari Game Reserve. The pace of life here is dictated by the demands of traditional cattle farming and crop production. Many of the villagers maintain fields on the Boteti River floodplain. The floodplain also provides good grazing for livestock during the dry season.

In the centre of the village is the colonial-style Bailey's Store, started by Robert Archibald Bailey, a trader who came to the former Bechuanaland Protectorate (now the Republic of Botswana) in the late nineteenth century. He established his first trading store at Old Palapye, about 20 kilometres east of the present-day town of Palapye. Here he sold an eclectic array of goods: weapons, including muzzle-loaders and single-shot Martini-Henry rifles, gunpowder, ammunition, blankets and clothes,

A tuck shop in Rakops sells basic foodstuffs.

Baileys Store has a long history of trading in Rakops.

all of which had to be transported from South Africa to Palapye by ox wagon. As demand for his goods grew in the region, Bailey opened a succession of shops – in Maun, Letlhakane, Mopipi, Rakops, Makalamabedi and Gweta. All of these stores, with the exception of those in Maun and Gweta, are still in operation today.

Local people also sold their cattle to these stores. The animals were then transported to abattoirs in Johannesburg and even the Copperbelt in the former Northern Rhodesia (now Zambia).

There are more facilities for travellers in Rakops than in other villages in the area. Basic supplies can be obtained at the village's only supermarket and a few general dealers. The fuel station is close to the main road, but fuel is not always available. There are also puncture-repair services, with one of them also selling basic motor spares. Other amenities include a car wash, a government hospital and an internet café.

## Places to stay

### Xere Motel

The Xere Motel can be found along the Letlhakane–Maun road, between the first and second turnoffs to Rakops. The motel features a selection of comfortably furnished en-suite chalets, equipped with air conditioning and TV. There is a restaurant and bar, although only soft drinks are available.

### Rakops River Lodge

Located 7 kilometres north of Rakops along the Boteti River, just off the Letlhakane–Maun road, the Rakops River Lodge consists of thatched chalets, with en-suite bathrooms, air conditioning and a TV. The camp site has nine shady sites with wooden tables and benches, traditional courtyards and electricity. There is a communal ablution block. The lodge's restaurant serves a full breakfast; other meals are prepared on request. Bar facilities are also available.

### Matsaudi Camp Site

Situated approximately 2 kilometres outside Rakops, this is a rustic camp site. Ablutions consist of open-air bucket showers and flush toilets. Dome tents, with beds, mattresses and bedding, are also available for hire.

## KHUMAGA

Travelling north from Rakops to Khumaga, you will see the grasslands gently giving way to sandveld and open woodland dominated by magnificent specimens of camel thorn. This village marks another gateway to the Makgadikgadi and Nxai Pans National Park. There are very few facilities here for visitors, although there are a handful of tuck shops and a bakery.

## Places to stay

### Meno a Kwena Camp

From their lofty perch atop a cliff overlooking the Boteti River, Meno a Kwena Camp's ten guest tents offer a combination of stylish home comforts and spectacular game viewing. Located between Khumaga and Motopi, on the boundary of the Makgadikgadi and Nxai Pans National Park, this tented lodge is the ideal place from which to observe a procession of wild animals. Between May and October, its lofty heights

NATURAL SELECTION

Perched on a hilltop, the tents at Meno a Kwena Camp have expansive views across the Boteti River.

afford front-row seats to Botswana's annual zebra and blue wildebeest migration.

Each tent has its own veranda and en-suite bathroom, and the décor is rustic and understated. Two of the nine units are large enough, with interleading tents, to accommodate families with children. Sand paths leading through the bush connect the living quarters to the capacious lounge, bar and dining tents. Other facilities include a swimming pool carved from rock and a well-stocked library.

### Leroo La Tau

The luxury lodge Leroo La Tau is situated about 9 kilometres northwest of Khumaga village, on the western bank of the Boteti River. It features 12 thatched and glass-fronted suites, each one built on a raised wooden platform to take full advantage of the glorious views across the river towards the Makgadikgadi and Nxai Pans National Park. The landscape is even more verdant in summer.

Facilities include a lounge, bar and restaurant, a swimming pool and a game-viewing hide that overlooks the river.

A variety of animals come to the Boteti to slake their thirst, including springbok, blue wildebeest, kudu and impala. Where antelope gather, so do their predators, and lions, cheetah and hyenas are likely to be spotted. A small population of hippos lives in the deep pools in the riverbed.

### Boteti River Camp

Situated on the outskirts of Khumaga village and close to the Khumaga entrance gate to the Makgadikgadi and Nxai Pans National Park, the Boteti River Camp (formerly Tiaan's Camp) is a good place to stay for a night or two. Accommodation is in en-suite chalets with air conditioning or in elevated tents with an open-air shower. A camping ground offers spacious shaded sites with water taps, electricity and shared ablutions.

Guests at Leroo La Tau enjoy sunrise over the Boteti River.

DESERT AND DELTA SAFARIS

# Things to do

## Mopipi, Rakops and Khumaga

### Exploring Rysana Pan

**MOPIPI:** About 26 kilometres southeast from Mopipi, along the road to Letlhakane, is a turnoff to Rysana Pan. The turnoff is marked by two large concrete water tanks on the northern side of the road. From here, a 10-kilometre track runs north through attractive mopane bush to the pan, where, depending on the time of year, flamingoes may be observed. The track is suitable for 2x4 pickup trucks and 4x4 vehicles only. Camping is permitted along the edge of the pan.

### Visiting fossil footprints

**MOPIPI:** To the west of Rysana Pan is Xanikaga, a protected palaeontological site that can be accessed from the road between Letlhakane and Mopipi. This site is today a shallow, dry pan, consisting of exposed sediments dating back to about 10,000 years ago, when Lake Makgadikgadi began to dry out. Preserved in these sediments is a rare set of fossilized tracks of animals that roamed the Makgadikgadi area during Plio-Pleistocene times, between about 5 million and 12,000 years ago. With a little luck and perseverance, you may be able to differentiate between footprints made by various animals around the time that the lake dried up.

To reach Xanikaga, follow the road from Mopipi towards Orapa. The turnoff is some 14 kilometres east of Mopipi. From here, follow the track northwards to the site. Note that the distance is 17 kilometres and not 10 kilometres, as indicated on the sign. As there are no other signboards along the route, it is easy to get lost. If you do lose the way, ask for directions at the Machana veterinary gate (open 6am–10pm) or at any of the cattle posts dotted around the area.

The route requires a 2x4 pickup truck or a 4x4 and is not suitable for saloon cars. There are no facilities at Xanikaga.

### Cycling

**RAKOPS:** Bicycles are available for hire at Rakops River Lodge for use either in the lodge grounds or in the village.

### Cultural tours

**KHUMAGA:** Meno a Kwena Camp, Leroo La Tau and Boteti River Camp offer trips to Khumaga village for visitors who are keen to experience daily life in a traditional rural settlement.

### Game drives

**KHUMAGA:** Meno a Kwena Camp and Leroo La Tau offer guided game drives in the Makgadikgadi Pans section of the national park, while Boteti River Camp offers half- and full-day game drives in the Makgadikgadi and Nxai sections, respectively.

### Boat safaris

**KHUMAGA:** When there is sufficient water in the Boteti River, guests at both Meno a Kwena and Leroo La Tau can sign up for boat trips to see the wildlife up close.

DESERT AND DELTA SAFARIS

After good rains, it is possible to explore the Boteti River by boat.

# Mosu/Kaitshe Escarpment

## A window on the past

## CHAPTER 7

Along the southeastern margin of Sowa Pan, near the small village of Mosu, a steep rocky escarpment rises approximately a hundred metres above the surrounding landscape and extends for more than 20 kilometres to the east of the settlement. The Mosu/Kaitshe Escarpment, as it is known, is composed of some of the oldest sedimentary rocks on earth, deposited between 300 and 180 million years ago. The ridge itself probably formed at the beginning of the Cretaceous period, about 136 million years ago, as a result of uplifting of the land.

The escarpment constitutes a small window on the area's geological past, its steep cliffs revealing the layers of sediment that accumulated here over millions of years. Beginning at the base, the Tlapana mudstone was formed about 280 million years ago. It is overlaid by a succession of sediments: the Kautse beds followed by Mosu sandstone and the younger Ntane sandstone, which formed during the Jurassic, when the sands that were deposited by strong winds solidified into sandstone. Today, the Ntane sandstone is capped with a thick layer of calcrete.

But there is much more to this remote region than its fascinating geological past. Along the top of the escarpment and at its base are several archaeological sites – the ruins of stone-walled settlements – that shed some light on the history of human migration and habitation over millennia along Sowa Pan and the escarpment that marks its southern shoreline. The best known of these are Tlapana Ruin, just outside Mea, and the Mma Kgama and Kaitshe ruins, both national monuments, near Mosu.

In modern times, new settlements have been established in this region: Mosu, Mmatshumo, Makgaba, Mokubilo and Mea are some of the more prominent places here. Mosu, a traditional village with beautifully decorated rondavels, is the largest of the villages in the area, and the launch pad for many of the sights and activities that can be enjoyed in this part of the Makgadikgadi region. It lies 25 kilometres off the Francistown–Orapa road on the southern route to Lekhubu Island.

---

Overlooking Sowa Pan, the Mosu/Kaitshe Escarpment is both an important wilderness area and an exceptional archaeological heritage site.

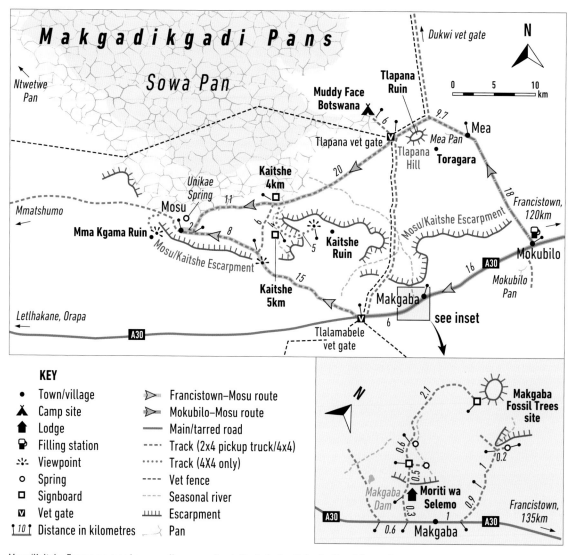

KEY

| | | | |
|---|---|---|---|
| • | Town/village | ▷ | Francistown–Mosu route |
| ⛺ | Camp site | ▷ | Mokubilo–Mosu route |
| 🏠 | Lodge | — | Main/tarred road |
| ⛽ | Filling station | - - - | Track (2x4 pickup truck/4x4) |
| ☀ | Viewpoint | ···· | Track (4X4 only) |
| ○ | Spring | - - - - | Vet fence |
| □ | Signboard | - - - | Seasonal river |
| Ⓥ | Vet gate | ⊥⊥⊥ | Escarpment |
| ↥10↥ | Distance in kilometres | ⟍⟍ | Pan |

Mosu/Kaitshe Escarpment and surrounding areas. Inset: Route to the Makgaba Fossil Trees site.

Few facilities are available in these villages, although Mosu has a puncture-repair service, a few tuck shops, a clinic and two general dealers. Items such as bread and fresh vegetables are very difficult to come by though.

# Prehistory

Humans, and animals, have been attracted by the bounty of the ancient Lake Makgadikgadi for millennia. Early Stone Age tools, such as handaxes, found along the Mosu/Kaitshe Escarpment suggest that early humans lived in the area between 1 million and 300,000 years ago. Stone tools created during the Middle and Later Stone Ages have also been found on and below the escarpment, and on Ntwetwe Pan, indicating that habitation occurred during drier periods as well. It is likely that the multiple springs along the base of the escarpment would have encouraged human settlement during times of scarce rainfall.

About 2,000 years ago, a transition from hunting and gathering to settled agriculture took place, and Later Stone Age people (San) living around Sowa Pan began to acquire livestock from Bantu-speaking farmers and herders living to the northeast in present-day Zimbabwe. This process accelerated when, around AD 400, the first Bantu-speaking farmers and herders began to move into the area, mainly along the Boteti River.

### Leopard's Kopje

It was only around AD 900 that the first Iron Age farmers, known as the Leopard's Kopje people, settled in the area south of Sowa Pan. The Leopard's Kopje people inhabited much of southwestern Zimbabwe, northeastern Botswana and the Limpopo River Valley in modern South Africa from about AD 900–1300. Their name is derived from the place where their pottery was first excavated at Thabazengwe, meaning 'kopje of the leopard', near Bulawayo in Zimbabwe. Some historians now believe that they were the ancestors of the Bakalanga who today live in the area between Francistown and the pans and are related to the Shona of Zimbabwe.

Several settlements developed along the top of the Mosu/Kaitshe Escarpment, many of which were occupied for long periods of time. To date, at least 12 settlements on the top of the escarpment have been surveyed. The wall

Kaitshe Ruin lies on the summit of the escarpment.

ruins of one such settlement, Kaitshe, probably marked the gateway to a village. Chert found in deposits here may have been traded for salt and game skins obtained from the San.

### Great Zimbabwe state

The southwestern corner of Sowa Pan marked the western extent of the Great Zimbabwe state, which lasted from about AD 1200–1450. The king, living at Great Zimbabwe (the ruins near present-day Masvingo in Zimbabwe), ruled over a vast territory from Sowa Pan in the west to Mozambique in the east, and from the Lotsane River in southern Botswana to the Zambezi River in the north – an area larger than modern Botswana. During this time, chiefs (akin to district governors) built residences on rocky hilltops, while the commoners erected their homes in the foothills and on the surrounding plains. There are two sites along the escarpment that date back to this time, both likely to have been the residences of chiefs: Mma Kgama Ruin near Mosu and the Tlapana Ruin just outside Mea.

The Mma Kgama Ruin is located on a 40-metre-high rocky promontory linked to the escarpment, some 3 kilometres west of Mosu. The site consists of several well-preserved stone-walled enclosures, up to 2 metres in height, as well as other artefacts, including the remains of hut floors and clay walls, stone platforms and pieces of pottery. The type of stone walling found at Mma Kgama also occurs at other Great Zimbabwe sites in the region; it was traditionally reserved for the residences of the elite, for example, a chief, his family and high-ranking members of the society.

The people who lived here most likely participated in a regional trade network that involved exchanging wares with local hunter-gatherer communities as well as with societies further away. Goods such as salt and animal hides would have been used to trade with people living to the east as far away as the Limpopo River Valley in modern-day South Africa.

The Mma Kgama Ruin near Mosu village is a national monument.

The Tlapana Ruin is situated on the summit of a flat-topped hill to the south of the Mea–Mosu track, 6 kilometres west of Mea village. It overlooks the southwestern corner of Sowa Pan. Three low stone walls, less well preserved than those at Mma Kgama Ruin, can be seen here.

## Fossils, springs and smaller pans

### Makgaba Fossil Trees

Along the southern edge of Sowa Pan, just below the Mosu/Kaishe Escarpment, is the Makgaba national monument, a protected palaeontological site that safeguards a collection of fossil trees that grew here between 250 and 240 million years ago. Recent research suggests that the fossil wood is of the species *Agathoxylon africanum*, which thrived in this part of southern Africa during the Triassic period.

The site is approximately 136 kilometres from Francistown along the Francistown–Orapa road and just north of the Moriti wa Selemo Adventures Bush Camp (outside Makgaba village), about 6 kilometres east of the Tlalamabele veterinary gate.

To reach the site, follow the track northwards from the signboard in the village (note that the track is suitable for 4x4s and 2x4 pickup trucks only). After about 3 kilometres, there is

another signboard. Leave your vehicle here and continue on foot along a small stream bed for a few hundred metres until you reach a fenced area, inside of which are some large chunks of petrified tree trunks.

Another fenced area, containing several pieces of petrified wood, is on the southern slope of the hill, immediately to the north.

### Natural springs

The perennial Unikae Spring is a natural outlet for water that drains from the Mosu/Kaitshe Escarpment. Rain falling on top of the escarpment flows downwards through the permeable sandstone and emerges as fresh, clear water from exposed rock at the northeastern end of Mosu village. Located behind the Mosu Primary School, the spring is a national monument, and is protected by a low stone wall.

A small dam has been built downstream for the villagers' livestock and horses. The spring's other regulars, a procession of doves, arrive in a flurry in the early morning to quench their thirst.

Some religious groups regard the spring as sacred and use its water for spiritual cleansing.

More springs are scattered along the grassland margins immediately north of Mosu. These are mostly seasonal and discharge less water. Some springs also occur along

Unikae Spring is protected from livestock by a low stone wall.

the escarpment near Makgaba village and Moriti wa Selemo Adventures Bush Camp on the outskirts of the village. One of these, the Simane mo Tshaa Spring, has cut a deep gorge into the escarpment.

## Pans

Dispersed along the southern limit of Sowa and Ntwetwe pans are several smaller pans, not all of which are relics of the ancient inland lake that once existed here.

Mokubilo Pan is one such pan and lies south of the small village from which it gets its name. A signposted track in the village runs southwards to the pan for 2 kilometres.

Unlike the nearby Sowa Pan, it is a more recent depression, filled with clay deposits rather than salt. The ancient Lake Makgadikgadi did not extend as far south as here, and the Mokubilo Pan was formed later by deflation – the removal of loose surface particles by the wind, resulting in the creation of shallow depressions. Subsequently, as water flowed into the pan, clay sediments were deposited here. As the pan is not saline, it is covered with grass, making it a good place for a picnic or for camping. Birdwatchers will be able to see large numbers of grey-backed sparrow-larks in the vicinity.

Just south of Mea village is a small salt flat known as Mea Pan. Of interest here is the Toragara site, a series of circular basin-like features in the sandstones. In Setswana, they are known as *megopo ya badimo*, meaning 'the bowls of the ancestors'. It is thought that the chemical composition of floodwater, together with large seasonal variations in both flooding and water chemistry, contributed to the formation of these unique rocks. A handful of springs occur along the margins of Mea Pan, and small flocks of flamingoes frequent the salt flat.

A small flock of flamingoes feed on crustaceans at Mea Pan.

# Things to do

## Self-guided walks

There are very few designated hiking trails at this end of Sowa Pan, but there are several unmarked paths that lead to places of interest in and around the villages and up to the top of the escarpment. Visitors are free to walk almost anywhere around these settlements, and there are hardly any fenced-off areas.

**MOSU VILLAGE:** Meander through Mosu village to view the traditional rondavels – their exterior walls are tinted with a range of colours, created by mixing natural colourants into the plaster. These are mostly sourced locally: red-brown from loam soils in the Dukwi area; grey from muddy river banks; pale green and white from calcrete; and black from charcoal or clay mixed with battery powder (used for the manganese that it contains).

Also visit the *kgotla* (tribal administration) where there are some eye-catching murals depicting the need to protect the local birdlife.

**MOSU/KAITSHE ESCARPMENT:** The spectacular views from the Mosu/Kaitshe Escarpment over Mosu village and the pan are ample reward for the effort of scaling this rocky slope. Take care when ascending the escarpment, as it requires scrambling over rocks, some of which are loose. A fence lies between the escarpment and the village; visitors may duck under it where it crosses gullies. An easy, well-marked path to the Mma Kgama Ruin at the top of the escarpment also offers good views of the surrounding landscape.

**UNIKAE WATER SPRING:** Also recommended is the walk north from Unikae Spring (vehicles may be left here) down to the grasslands along the edge of the pan. Walking in an easterly direction from the spring will take you to palm groves and springs. A short walk north of the springs will bring you to Sowa Pan itself.

## Self-guided drives

A popular route is from Mokubilo to Mosu via Mea. The well-graded gravel road from Mokubilo to Mea is suitable for saloon cars. At Mea, the road changes into a track, which requires skilled navigation in a 4x4 or 2x4 pickup truck. Drivers of saloon cars should not proceed beyond this point.

The track from Mea continues westwards through lovely scenery along the foot of the escarpment, meandering through areas of grassland and patches of woodland dotted with baobabs. After about 29 kilometres there is a signboard saying 'Kaitshe Escarpment 4km'. Follow the track to the left (suitable only for 4x4 vehicles), which leads to the Kaitshe Ruin. After 4 kilometres, turn left at the next signpost – indicating that Kaitshe Escarpment is 5 kilometres away – and follow the stony track to the viewpoint on the plateau where you can park your vehicle. The ruins are a few hundred metres from here and can be reached on foot.

## Guided drives and walks

Using your own vehicle, you may be able to arrange for a guide at the Makgaba *kgotla* to accompany you on outings during the week. On weekends, the owner of Moriti wa Selemo may either offer his services as a guide or

Spectacular views from the top of the escarpment take in woodlands, grassland and the desiccated fringes of Sowa Pan. The flooded pan can be seen in the distance.

recommend a knowledgeable local resident to join you on your excursion. Sights that can be seen in the area include the Makgaba tree fossils and the Mma Kgama Ruin.

## Land yachting

Botswana may be far from the sea, but that does not stop visitors from sailing a yacht on wheels on Sowa Pan. This activity is best undertaken in the dry season, from May to October, when the pan is free from moisture and the wind is strong enough – between 8 and 15 knots – to 'power' the yacht. For bookings, contact Moriti wa Selemo.

## Quad biking

Rides on the pan can be arranged through the owner of Moriti wa Selemo. There is also a 600-metre track adjacent to the camp, which is suitable for quad biking.

## Off-road biking, cycling and quad biking

Southern Sowa Pan is the scene of an action-packed weekend for off-road bikers and cyclists in July each year. The Makgadikgadi Moonlight Adventure, organized by Muddy Face Botswana, encompasses a series of races held under a full moon on Sowa Pan, some 15 kilometres west of Mea village.

The night races involve bikers stretching the limits of their endurance on 30-, 15- and 10-kilometre loops on the pan. There is also a short obstacle course, consisting of several natural and human-made hurdles that must be navigated by riders. Additional events include a separate loop designed for cyclists and races for quad bikers.

Accommodation is in tents, with visitors either pitching their own or hiring tents equipped with beds and bedding. Hot showers and toilets are available. Meals are for sale and a bar is open throughout the weekend.

To get to the venue, drive west from Mea along the Mea–Mosu track to the veterinary

checkpoint. From here, follow a track to the north for 6 kilometres until you reach the site.

The event is dependent on the weather, and will only take place if the pan is dry for at least 50 kilometres out from the southern shoreline.

The dry season provides the best conditions for land yachting.

The annual Makgadikgadi Moonlight Adventure is an opportunity for off-roaders of all kinds, from quad bikers (top) to motorcyclists (above), to demonstrate their skills.

## Vegetation

For a semiarid area, there is a surprising variety of plants in the vicinity of the escarpment. In the middle of Mosu village is a woodland dominated by fine specimens of the large, flat-topped umbrella thorn (*Vachellia tortilis*). Also look out for camel thorn (*Vachellia erioloba*) and bushveld albizia (*Albizia harveyi*) trees, characterized by distinctive brownish pods. Elsewhere in the village the vegetation consists of small mopane (*Colophospermum mopane*) bushes, which are most attractive in June and July when the leaves turn reddish brown. Some small shepherd's trees (*Boscia albitrunca*), with their distinctive pale grey to whitish trunks, also grow here.

Around the springs the vegetation is almost luxuriant, with sedges, bulrushes and groves of tall real fan palms (*Hyphaene petersiana*) relishing the conditions here.

Towards Sowa Pan the vegetation becomes more sparse. Notable species include the sesame bush (*Sesomothamnus lugardii*), with its smooth, brownish yellow underbark, and the magnificent African star-chestnut (*Sterculia africana*), identified by its attractive purplish peeling bark. About a kilometre north of Mosu is a small forest of these trees, which makes for a good camping spot. A clutch of small baobabs also grow here. Along the pan margins species such as hoodia (*Hoodia lugardii*) thrive among the thick grasses.

## Places to stay

**Moriti wa Selemo Adventures Bush Camp**
Near the village of Makgaba, 136 kilometres west of Francistown along the Orapa road, is Moriti wa Selemo Adventures Bush Camp, the only formal accommodation option in the area. There is also a signboard to the camp in the village itself.

Real fan palms thrive around a spring just north of Mosu village.

Accommodation at Moriti wa Selemo Adventures Bush Camp is in attractive wood-and-thatch cabins or dome tents.

This delightful shady establishment is situated in a deciduous woodland at the edge of the escarpment (*Moriti wa Selemo* means 'summer shade' in Setswana).

Lodgings are in cosy, dome-shaped thatched chalets or in large dome tents equipped with beds, mattresses and bedding. There is also a well-shaded camp site with a communal ablution block. Each stand has its own tap, braai and electrical power point.

The restaurant and bar are in an attractive stone building covered by a high thatched roof. All meals are on request.

# Getting there

There are two approaches to Mosu, one from the east, the other from the west.

### Route 1: Francistown to Mosu

**Total distance:** 167 kilometres; **Time:** 2–2.5 hours
From Francistown's city centre, take the A3 road to Maun. After 8 kilometres, take the tarred A30 road westwards towards Orapa. Continue for 134 kilometres until you reach the Tlalamabele veterinary gate. Once through the gate, take the track signposted 'Mosu' to the right. After 13 kilometres you will be rewarded with a fine view of Sowa Pan from the top of the Mosu/Kaitshe Escarpment. Now follow the track down the escarpment (it is not very steep); once at the bottom, the land becomes flatter and the track passes through mopane scrub. Continue along this track until you reach Mosu. Although this route can be travelled in a saloon car (with great care), it is best to tackle it in a 4x4 or a 2x4 pickup truck.

### Route 2: Letlhakane to Mosu

**Total distance:** 76 kilometres; **Time:** 1.5 hours
Take the main tarred road out of Letlhakane in a northerly direction for 12 kilometres until you reach a major crossroads. Cross over the Francistown–Orapa road and continue for 22 kilometres until you reach the village of Mmatshumo. In the middle of the village, just beyond the offices of the Gaing O Community Trust, take the tarred turnoff to the right. This road leads to Mosu, some 42 kilometres further. The tar ends after a few kilometres, giving way to a road with a hard calcrete surface.

Take care when driving along this road. Although it can be negotiated with a saloon car, the surface can become corrugated, especially if it has not been recently graded. There may also be potholes after unusually heavy rains.

# Lekhubu Island

## Refuge of granite

## CHAPTER 8

Although it is not the only rocky outcrop on the Makgadikgadi Pans, Lekhubu Island is the most dramatic, and one of a few composed of igneous rock. Seen from afar, its granitic monoliths appear to rise from the lakebed, keeping watch over a shimmering sea of salt that stretches as far as the eye can see. Large baobabs find purchase in the soil between the boulders, their contorted branches casting crooked shadows over the scattered rocks and the grassy fringes of Sowa Pan. As the sun sets, the harsh light of the day gives way to the soft glow of the moon, and the rocks and trees parade their dark silhouettes against a star-studded sky.

This ancient and evocative place, more commonly known as Kubu, is located at the southwestern corner of Sowa Pan. The nearest villages are Mosu, 40 kilometres to the southeast of the island, and Mmatshumo, 45 kilometres to the southwest. The mining town of Letlhakane lies some 80 kilometres to the south.

## Prehistory

Lekhubu Island has attracted humans for millenia. The site was intermittently occupied by hunter-gatherers who may have used it as a hunting ground during wetter periods when animals were relatively abundant.

From around AD 1200, the island was settled by Iron Age people and there is some evidence that they exchanged salt for other goods with traders from what is today eastern Botswana and northeastern South Africa. Objects found here that date back to this time include pottery shards and beads made of ostrich-egg shells.

On the southern shore of the island – behind the information board you will see on arrival – is a crescent-shaped wall made of loosely packed stones. The remains of an ancient enclosure, it is about 1.2 metres high and several hundred metres long. Its purpose is unknown, but archaeologists have suggested that the site may have served as an initiation centre.

Scattered across the island are some 450 stone cairns, many about 1–1.5 metres in diameter and up

A mass of granite boulders, ancient baobab trees and grassy patches, Lekhubu Island has been a shelter for human beings for millennia.

Ancient stone walls (above) and stone cairns associated with initiation ceremonies (inset) are evidence of human habitation on the island more than 600 years ago. A deep cleft in the rocks serves as a cave where local residents can make offerings to their ancestors (right).

to 50 centimetres in height (good examples may be seen between the camp site and the survey beacon). They, too, may be associated with initiation rites since they resemble similar structures found at initiation sites throughout the former Great Zimbabwe state. Some archaeologists are of the opinion that this provides evidence for the argument that the area came under the influence of Great Zimbabwe, a Shona kingdom that flourished in southern Africa between AD 1200 and 1450 (see also Chapter 7).

At the eastern end of the island, among massive granite boulders, is a cave that is used by local people for ritual ceremonies. It serves as a rain shrine and as a place where people can leave offerings, such as snuff and coins, to appease their ancestors. These offerings are sacred and should not be touched or removed.

To preserve its cultural history and natural resources, Lekhubu has been declared a national monument.

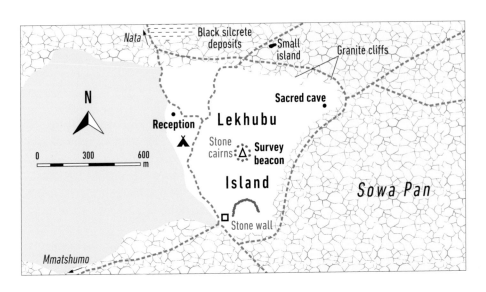

KEY

✕ Camp site
□ Signboard
----- Track (2x4 pickup truck/ 4x4)
Pan
Grasslands

Lekhubu Island and surrounding area.

# Geology

Lekhubu Island is a granite outcrop about one kilometre long; at its highest point it rises some 20 metres above the surrounding pan (this point is marked by a prominent survey beacon). Granite is an igneous rock formed by the cooling of molten magma several kilometres below the surface of the earth. The softer Karoo sedimentary rocks that once overlaid the granite were gradually eroded, allowing the hard igneous rock to be exposed at the surface. In the northeastern section of the island, the granite has formed mini cliffs; elsewhere, it has been eroded into giant boulders and smaller rocks.

The coarse-grained nature of the granite allows for easy identification of some of the minerals present in the rock: on close inspection you can see colourless quartz, whitish plagioclase feldspar, biotite (also known as black mica) and the distinctive pink crystals of orthoclase feldspar.

Several veins of crystallized quartz and orthoclase feldspar crisscross the granite. These mineral veins – some at least 30 centimetres wide – were formed by the intrusion of hot liquids into the already solidified granite. In some parts of the world, quartz veins contain valuable gold deposits, but, alas, there is no quick fortune to be made here – this is no Klondike or Witwatersrand!

African star-chestnut trees dwarf the island's massive boulders.

Distinctive veins of crystallized quartz and orthoclase feldspar crisscross the granite on Lekhubu Island.

Pebbles, rounded by wave action, form part of a fossil beach at the crest of Lekhubu Island.

The area around Lekhubu Island was once covered by a vast inland sea (see Chapter 2). Evidence of the existence of this mega lake – Lake Makgadikgadi – can be seen at the summit of the island, in the vicinity of the survey beacon. Greyish-white granite pebbles, some smooth and rounded and others oval-shaped, have accumulated here along an ancient beach, formed when the shoreline periodically stood at 920 metres above sea level, between 25,000 and 10,000 years ago. Given that the altitude of Sowa Pan is 890 metres, it is likely that the lake would have reached a depth of at least 30 metres.

Conversely, at intervals when the water levels were much higher – up to 945 metres above sea level – the rocky outcrop and the beach would simply have disappeared under the waves.

As you approach Lekhubu Island from Mmatshumo, you will see recent deposits of silcrete on the pan surface. Although the silcrete is primarily black in colour, it also has a greenish hue, due to the presence of the green mineral glauconite. Along the pan margins, the silcrete is well bedded, appearing in alternating greenish and greenish-black layers.

The land along the island margins slopes gently towards the pan before flattening out. Here the earth is covered with greyish sandy soils that are calcareous and contain calcrete, formed after the drying up of the lake.

## Vegetation

The centre of the island is given over to open deciduous woodland. Baobabs (*Adansonia digitata*) dominate the landscape, and their bulbous branches and massive trunks make them easily identifiable. In winter, when the trees have shed their leaves, the

The salt-tolerant grass species *Odyssea paucinervis* grows along the perimeter of the rocky island.

branches appear as a mass of roots pointing skyward, hence their nickname, the 'upside-down tree'. They come in all shapes and sizes: some are tall and slender in appearance, others are stubby and thick-stemmed, with the most hardy growing to enormous sizes. These trees are able to survive extremely harsh conditions, whether heat, cold, drought, flood or fire, and the most robust can have a life span of several thousand years – some specimens on the island are estimated to be more than 2,000 years old.

Baobabs make good subjects for photography – try shooting them as the setting sun paints them with shades of red or orange. In the dry season, the bare trees make good silhouettes at sunrise and sunset and on moonlit nights.

Other deciduous trees include the African star-chestnut (*Sterculia africana*) and the marula (*Sclerocarya birrea*). The African star-chestnut has a distinctive purplish bark that peels off to reveal a cream-white underbark. It is easily identified by its large olive-green leaves, divided into between three and five pointed lobes, small green flowers, and golden, boat-shaped fruits. The marula tree is famous for its nutritious fruit, used in a wide range of products from alcohol to body lotion. The tree has a well-developed crown and its outer bark peels off to give it a grey mottled appearance.

Bush savanna occurs along the margins of the island. This vegetation type consists of mainly smaller umbrella thorn (*Vachellia tortilis*) and purplepod clusterleaf (*Terminalia prunioides*) bushes – the latter preferring the more calcareous soils found here. The pan shoreline, however, is the habitat of only one species, the salt-tolerant grass *Odyssea paucinervis*.

## Wildlife

Do not expect to see much wildlife on Lekhubu Island – most people come here simply to admire the landscape and savour the atmosphere. Even so, there *is* evidence of animal life on the island and surrounding salt pan, and you may occasionally see brown hyena, jackal, impala, springbok and gemsbok.

But smaller mammals, too, may be observed. Near the reception building at the camp site, springhares have created large burrows in the sandy soil. Their common name is somewhat misleading, as they are in fact classified as rodents. They live underground during the

A rare sight in the vicinity of Lekhubu Island, the brown hyena is largely a solitary animal.

The camp site is dotted with multiple burrows in which springhares spend the day to escape the heat.

day to escape the heat and are active only at night. Although they may resemble hares, they behave more like miniature kangaroos, bounding and hopping on their hind legs. Smaller burrows in the vicinity are probably made by other rodents such as rats.

## Birdlife

Lekhubu may not be a twitcher's paradise – there is simply not enough surface water to sustain a large variety of birds here – but a day out will nevertheless gratify most birdwatchers. Birds regularly observed at the camp site include red-eyed bulbuls, sparrows, glossy starlings and violet-eared waxbills. A speciality of the island, the eye-catching waxbills have violet patches on their cheeks, a blue band across the forehead and a red bill.

Black and pied crows are a common sight, especially in the vicinity of the baobabs where their large bowl-shaped nests, composed of twigs and sticks, are conspicuous in the crowns of these trees. Western barn owls also occur here, as do lilac-breasted rollers and purple rollers.

The island's rocks are stained with fossilized guano of birds that frequented the ancient Lake Makgadikgadi – an indication that birdlife here was once prolific. You can imagine darters, cormorants, pelicans and African fish eagles spending their days perching on trees or hunting for fish in the waters that once lapped the shores of the island.

# Things to do

### Self-guided hikes

Although there are no marked trails in the area, visitors are free to walk anywhere on the island. An easy ramble is the 3-kilometre walk along the perimeter of the island, past the sacred cave and stone wall remains. Another popular walk, a few hundred metres in distance, leads from the camp site to the fossil beach (marked by the summit beacon), from where there are good views across the pan. Walkers should wear good shoes, as the terrain is rocky with loose stones in some places.

Although they are rarely seen, keep an eye out for snakes. Crevices are the preferred habitat of rock pythons.

The remains of an ancient stone wall can be seen on a ramble along the perimeter of Lekhubu Island.

### Guided hikes

The Gaing O Community Trust organizes guided half-day hikes at very reasonable rates. Email the Trust in advance to make the necessary arrangements.

### Charity hikes

The Gaborone-based YCare Charitable Trust aims to raise money for charitable organizations in Botswana. To achieve this goal, it organizes two annual walking events on the Makgadikgadi Pans, both starting and finishing at Mosu village. All proceeds raised from these events are given to worthy community-based projects.

Eager hikers make their way to Lekhubu Island.

Hikers get a close-up view of Lekhubu Island's ancient rocks.

The three-day Makgadikgadi Pans Day Walk is held during the President's Day long weekend in mid-July. Participants spend the first night camping on the outskirts of Mosu before setting off the next day on the first hike of the weekend – a 45-kilometre stretch to Lekhubu Island. The rest of the weekend is spent on the island, which serves as a base for additional activities, including a meander to nearby Little Kubu Island or a guided tour of Lekhubu Island itself. The final day sees everyone walking back to Mosu.

The night walk is held over a weekend in late August. On arrival at Mosu, participants hike during the night under a full moon to Lekhubu Island. After a few hours' rest, they are taken on a guided day tour of the island before returning to Mosu that evening.

Participants in both events are provided with accommodation in dome tents, buffet-style meals and medical support. Walkers are given packed lunches, and water is supplied along the route.

### Guided 4x4 tours and safaris

Gweta Lodge and other establishments offer guided 4x4 trips to Lekhubu Island. These can range from day trips to multiday safaris. Since these tours are usually dependent on the availability of suitable guides, it is best to contact a tour operator or the lodge you will be staying at to make the necessary arrangements.

An off-road vehicle is essential for visiting Lekhubu Island. A guided 4x4 trip, on the other hand, has the benefit of a stress-free exploration of this wilderness area.

# Places to stay

### Lekhubu Island Camp Site

Lekhubu Island is managed by the Gaing O Community Trust. Based in Mmatshumo village, it was established in 1997 to ensure the sustainable use of the community's natural resources, including Lekhubu Island. Proceeds from the camp site and other organized activities are reinvested in the development of the village. In addition to sustaining the eco-tourism venture at Lekhubu Island, the Trust has helped build homes for destitute people and has paid for the school uniforms and shoes of some of the village's poorest children.

There are 13 basic pitches in the camp site, some located along the margin of the pan and others set in the shade of large trees further inland. All afford spectacular views of the surrounding landscape. If these sites are full, visitors may obtain permission to camp in an 'overflow' area nearby. There is no ablution block and only pit latrines are available.

Campers must bring their own fuel, food and water, as there are no other facilities on the island.

It is advisable to pay camping fees in advance by bank transfer. On proof of payment, the Trust will email you a voucher, which you need to present on arrival at the camping site. Alternatively, you can call ahead to ascertain whether the Trust will accept a cash payment on arrival (there are no credit card facilities).

### Makgadikgadi Adventure Camp

Ten kilometres to the south of Thabatshukudu village, at the Tswagong veterinary gate, lies Makgadikgadi Adventure Camp, a self-catering establishment that can be used as a base to explore the nearby Lekhubu Island. It has camp sites, an ablution block (with flush toilets and hot showers), a bar and a communal braai area. Six bow tents with beds and two cottage tents with beds and full bedding are available for hire.

Lekhubu Island presents myriad opportunities for sunset photography.

Makgadikgadi Adventure Camp takes visitors on guided trips to Lekhubu Island and Sowa Pan.

The camp offers visitors a range of activities, including guided sunset and sunrise drives onto Sowa Pan; guided bush walks to view local flora and fauna; horseback rides, lasting from a few hours to all day; and stargazing.

The tracks to the adventure camp are suitable for 4x4 vehicles and 2x4 pickup trucks with good ground clearance, but not for saloon cars.

## Getting there

There are two approaches to Lekhubu Island from the south – the first is from Letlhakane and the second from Mosu village. Lekhubu Island can also be accessed from the north along the Nata–Maun road.

### Route 1 – Letlhakane to Lekhubu Island

**Total distance:** 80 kilometres; **Time:** 2–2.5 hours
From Letlhakane, proceed to Mmatshumo. In the middle of Mmatshumo – just beyond

the Gaing O Community Trust office – you will see the turnoff to the tarred road to Mosu on the right (this is the road described under Route 2, p. 97). Continue past the Mosu turnoff, proceeding straight for 50 metres until you reach a sign saying 'Kubu Island 45km'. Here the tarred road becomes a wide track; continue along this track for 5 kilometres until you reach a lookout platform on the right-hand side, offering spectacular views of Sowa Pan in the distance. From here the track descends a calcrete escarpment and narrows through a flat section of mopane scrub for 9 kilometres. Bumpy and stony at times, with deep ruts, this section of the track is perhaps the most difficult along the route. The old lake deposits here are also very fine and your vehicle will churn up clouds of very fine dust. After approximately 3 kilometres from the viewing platform, you will pass another sign to Kubu. Note that the track from here on repeatedly

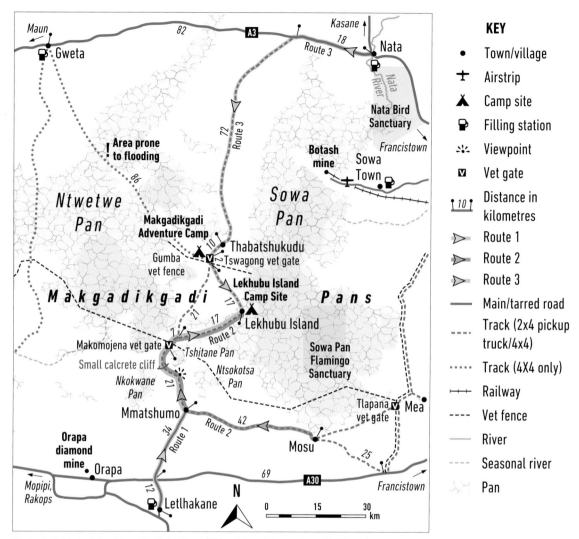

Routes to Lekhubu Island from the Nata–Maun (A3) and Francistown–Orapa (A30) roads.

divides into two over the next few kilometres. It does not matter which branch you take, since the tracks rejoin a little further on.

Nine kilometres from the viewing platform, a track leads off to the right. Follow it for a short distance until you reach a small pan. Continue across the pan; after 7 kilometres you will reach a veterinary fence. Pass through the Makomojena veterinary gate here (open daily from 6am to 10pm) and continue across the open grasslands for another 7 kilometres to reach a fork in the track. The left fork leads

to Makgadikgadi Adventure Camp. Take the right fork (a sign here reads 'Kubu 17km') and follow it across Sowa Pan for 17 kilometres until you reach the island. This last section is by far the easiest part of the trip, as driving on the pan surface is almost like driving on a good tarred road.

If the small pan before the veterinary gate is wet, it may be advisable to take a detour that crosses a much smaller part of the pan than the main track. Backtrack to the end of the mopane scrub section. Instead of turning

There are several routes to Lekhubu Island, all requiring drivers to negotiate a range of dirt tracks.

right (as described above), continue straight for 4 kilometres until you reach a sign to Kubu. Turn right here to reach Makomojena veterinary gate after 3 kilometres. Continue to Lekhubu Island along the main track, following the directions given above.

Although a 4x4 vehicle is recommended, you will probably not have to engage four-wheel drive along this route – at least not in the dry season. It is also possible to reach Lekhubu Island in a 2x4 pickup truck with good ground clearance in the dry season. It is best to avoid doing this journey in a saloon car – on a recent trip to the island, the author passed a car that had broken down 18 kilometres short of the island, its back wheels twisted after one of the shock absorbers broke.

## ROUTE 2 – Mosu to Lekhubu Island

**Total distance:** 87 kilometres; **Time:** 2–2.5 hours
Drive through Mosu, along the road from the Tlalamabele veterinary fence, until you reach a clinic on the left-hand side of the road (also see the map in Chapter 7 for directions from the Tlalamabele veterinary fence to Mosu.) Turn right at the T-junction and continue for 42 kilometres until you reach Mmatshumo. Here the road ends at another T-junction; turn

right at the junction and after 50 metres you will see a signpost saying 'Kubu Island 45km'. From here, follow the directions to Lekhubu Island given in Route 1 above.

## ROUTE 3 – Nata–Maun road to Lekhubu Island

**Total distance:** 119 kilometres; **Time:** 2.5–3 hours
From Nata, drive westwards for 18 kilometres along the Maun road. At the green road sign saying 'Kubu 91km' (there is also another turnoff at 26 kilometres), turn left and follow the track for about 72 kilometres until you reach the small village of Thabatshukudu. From here, you will have your first good view of Sowa Pan to the east. Continue along the track for another 10 kilometres until you reach Tswagong veterinary gate where you will pass Makgadikgadi Adventure Camp. Continue for another 2 kilometres until you see a track leading off to the left. Take this track, and after 17 kilometres you will reach the island.

Another route leads southeastwards from Gweta to the Tswagong veterinary gate. This 86-kilometre track is for adventure seekers only and should be approached with caution since it is subject to flooding where it crosses Ntwetwe Pan.

# Nata Bird Sanctuary

## A haven for waterbirds

## CHAPTER 9

Located on Sowa Pan, the Nata Bird Sanctuary covers an area of 230 square kilometres. The reserve protects the northeastern section of Sowa Pan, the surrounding grasslands and the Nata River Delta, and serves as a haven for the more than 378 bird species, including the globally threatened lesser flamingo, that gather here. Since more than 900 bird species occur in the entire southern Africa, the reserve is indeed rich in birdlife, earning it a reputation as one of the premier birdwatching destinations on the subcontinent. It is also part of the Makgadikgadi Pans Important Bird and Biodiversity Area (IBA), one of twelve such areas in Botswana. The IBA programme is a worldwide initiative aimed at the conservation of globally important birding areas.

Nata Bird Sanctuary lies along the tarred Nata–Francistown road. It is 170 kilometres from Francistown, while Nata village is a further 20 kilometres to the northwest. The sanctuary's location makes it an ideal stopover on the long journey to the Okavango Delta or Chobe National Park.

## History

The area occupied by the bird sanctuary was formerly used by the residents of Nata village and neighbouring settlements for grazing and watering their livestock. However, in 1988, the Nata Conservation Committee, with the assistance of the Kalahari Conservation Society and Nata Lodge, agreed to establish a conservation area to protect the breeding sites of migratory birds and the ecosystems of Sowa Pan, the Nata River Delta and the surrounding grasslands.

Nata Bird Sanctuary opened its gates to the public in 1993. A non-profit community operation, it is managed by the Nata Conservation Trust whose trustees include representatives from four surrounding settlements: Nata, Sepako, Mmanxotae and Maposa. Income generated from entrance, camping and other fees is used for the development of these villages.

The Botswana government believes that community-based natural resource management can play an important role in sustainable rural development. For this reason, local community trusts, such as the one in Nata, have been set up in different

Formerly a place where cattle came to graze, the northeastern end of Sowa Pan has been turned into a bird sanctuary designed to protect resident and migratory birds, such as these great white pelicans.

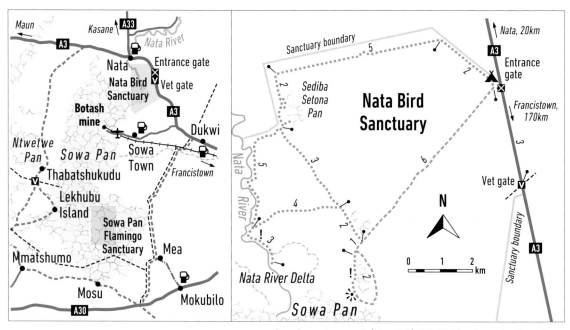

Sowa Pan and surrounds (above left); Nata Bird Sanctuary, showing main off-roading tracks (above right).

## KEY

| | | | |
|---|---|---|---|
| • | Town/village | ---·--- | Track (any vehicle) |
| ✛ | Airstrip | - - - | Track (2x4 pickup truck/4x4) |
| ⚑ | Camp site | ······ | Track (4X4 only) |
| ⛽ | Filling station | +-+-+ | Railway |
| ☀ | Viewpoint | - - - - | Vet fence |
| ⊠ | Entrance gate | —— | River |
| Ⓥ | Vet gate | - - - | Seasonal river |
| †10† | Distance in kilometres | ⌇⌇ | Pan |
| —— | Main/tarred road | | |

The trees along Nata River give way to grass where the river discharges into Sowa Pan, visible in the distance.

parts of northern Botswana, with the twin aims of preserving the local environment and using the proceeds of tourism and other ventures for the benefit of local people.

Nata Bird Sanctuary is open daily from 7am–7pm, but may be closed temporarily during periods of extensive flooding.

## Vegetation

The area around the bird sanctuary's entrance gate and camp site is dominated by mopane scrub, knob thorns (*Senegalia nigrescens*) and baobabs (*Adansonia digitata*). Travelling in a southerly direction towards the pan, you will enter the grasslands, where prickly salt grass (*Odyssea paucinervis*) appears in abundance alongside *Hoodia lugardii* and mopane aloes (*Aloe littoralis*). Tumbleweed (*Ammocharis coronica*) grows along the verges of some of the tracks; when in bloom it produces large white flowers.

Closer to the pan are some small patches of flooded grasslands where tall reeds grow. The pan itself – constituting 45 per cent of the sanctuary – sustains

Knob thorn and baobab trees throw long shadows over the camp site in the Nata Bird Sanctuary.

## Places to stay

### Nata Bird Sanctuary Camp Site

There is a pleasant camp site close to the entrance gate. The pitches are spacious and shady and are equipped with a braai stand, concrete table and benches, power points and an electric light. Communal facilities include a thatched ablution block with flush toilets and hot showers. There are six sites, three of which are named after local indigenous trees: Mowana (baobab), Mokoba (knob thorn) and Motswiri (leadwood). Brochures, including a map, may be available at Reception.

Plans are under way to construct chalets adjacent to the camp site and two lodges in the sanctuary. A bush camp site will also be set up nearer to the pan.

## Getting there

From Francistown, travel 170 kilometres along the Francistown–Maun (A3) road until you reach a veterinary fence with a communications tower nearby. From here, continue for another 3 kilometres until you reach the entrance gate to the Nata Bird Sanctuary on your left. The reception office is at the gate. Nata village lies a further 20 kilometres north along this road.

**The following facilities are available along the road between Francistown and Nata:**
- **Sebina crossroads (50 kilometres from Francistown):** One filling station with a store and takeaway.
- **Mosetse (116 kilometres from Francistown):** Vehicle- and puncture-repair service at Mosetse Brigades.
- **Dukwi (130 kilometres from Francistown):** A filling station and store.

In the distance, dust devils race across the sun-baked pan near the Nata Bird Sanctuary.

# Makgadikgadi and Nxai Pans National Park

## A wilderness of hidden treasures

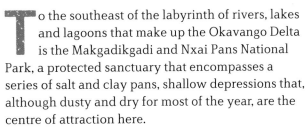

## CHAPTER 10

To the southeast of the labyrinth of rivers, lakes and lagoons that make up the Okavango Delta is the Makgadikgadi and Nxai Pans National Park, a protected sanctuary that encompasses a series of salt and clay pans, shallow depressions that, although dusty and dry for most of the year, are the centre of attraction here.

Ntwetwe Pan makes up about one-fifth of the Makgadigadi Pans, but only its western tip and a splatter of smaller pans along its fringe are included in the park. To the north, the Nxai Pan Complex, which incorporates the Kudiakam and Kgama Kgama pans, forms the nucleus of the Nxai Pan section.

Originally two separate protected areas, the Makgadikgadi and Nxai Pan reserves were combined to form a single national park in 1992. The Makgadikgadi Pans National Park was initially declared a game reserve in 1970, followed by the establishment of the Nxai Pan National Park a year later. The boundaries of both wilderness areas were extended in 1992, so that they now form a single contiguous park, covering a total of almost 7,500 square kilometres.

The well-maintained Nata–Maun road bisects the park. A convenient thoroughfare for travellers heading straight towards the delta, the road is suitable for all manner of vehicles. Within the park, however, a 4x4 vehicle is essential. The tracks are sandy and narrow, requiring vehicles with good ground clearance and low range. The roads can become especially treacherous in the rainy season when the clay surface around the pans becomes difficult to navigate.

The park is open to visitors all year round. The best time to explore the sanctuary is during the dry season, from May through to November, when the animals, desperate for water, cluster around the remaining water holes and pools to slake their thirst, making them more conspicuous than at any other time of the year. The wet season, from November to March, holds its own attractions: the Boteti River, along the western boundary of the park, becomes a lush haven

ONDREJ PROSICK/SHUTTERSTOCK

Storm clouds gather in the distance as a herd of gemsbok graze on the sweet grasses that blanket Nxai Pan.

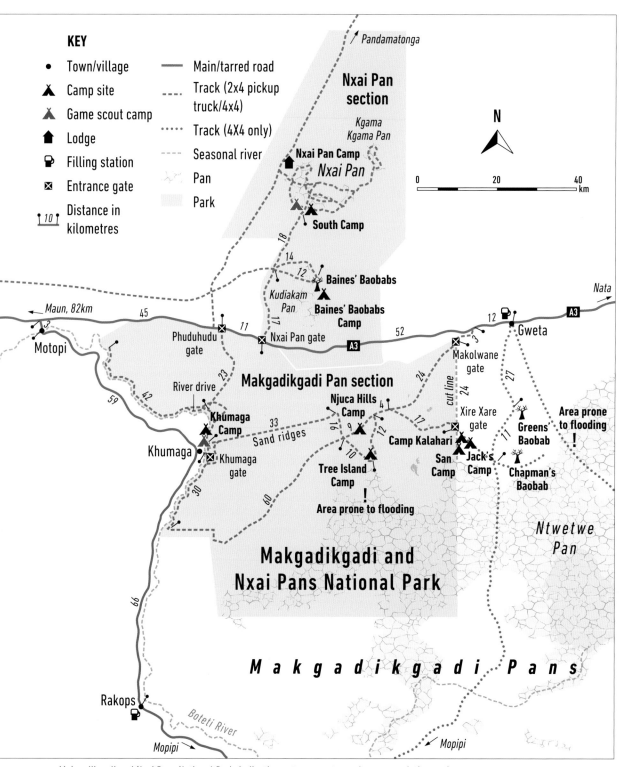

Makgadikgadi and Nxai Pans National Park, indicating entrance gates and accommodation options.

for birds and mammals, while the smaller pans and surrounding areas in the Nxai Pan section transform into a wonderland of shimmering water and green grasslands.

## Geology

The terrain here is mostly flat, the plain covered with Kalahari sands and occasionally punctuated by fossilized sand ridges and dunes. The most discernable of these rises, Njuca Hills, lies to the north of Ntwetwe Pan. Rising from the surrounding grasslands, the hills afford a 360-degree view over the surrounding area, serving as an excellent game-viewing spot.

Nxai Pan consists of blackish clay, and small, low-lying calcrete ridges occur in its vicinity. Like most of the pans in the park, it is a remnant of the ancient Lake Makgadikgadi, which at one time covered all of the Okavango Delta, the pans of the Makgadikgadi, the Mababe

Depression, Nxai Pan and Lake Ngami (see Chapter 2). Most of these ancient fossil pans are permanently covered with grass and dotted with acacia trees. Scattered among the grasses are shallow depressions that hold water during the rainy season.

## Vegetation

The vegetation in the park is typical of the Kalahari bush savanna, with grasses, bushes and trees growing in sandy soils. The dominant grass species here are three-awned grass (*Aristida meridionalis*), broom love grass (*Eragrostis pallens*) and silky Bushman grass (*Stipagrostis uniplumis*), all of which provide grazing for the herds of antelope that descend on the area following the first rains.

The most common small tree is the silver terminalia (*Terminalia sericea*), while the camel thorn (*Vachellia erioloba*) represents the most

MATHIAS SUNKE/SHUTTERSTOCK

A short distance from Kudiakam Pan is Baines' Baobabs Camp, its stands shaded by the massive deciduous trees from which it gets its name. Dry for most of the year, this fossil pan is transformed into an oasis during the rainy season.

common bush-like species in the area. Other species include sickle bush (*Dichrostachys cinerea*), Kalahari bauhinia (*Bauhinia petersiana*) and Kalahari currant (*Rhus tenuinervis*). Groves of real fan palms (*Hyphaene petersiana*) grow between the Nata–Maun road and Ntwetwe Pan; elsewhere, isolated stands of palms tower over the landscape.

Dense riverine woodland occurs along the eastern bank of the Boteti River. Unlike the bare and overgrazed western bank, which lies outside the park, the eastern bank is tightly packed with species such as camel thorn, buffalo thorn (*Ziziphis mucronata*), black thorn (*Senegalia mellifera*) and leadwood (*Combretum imberbe*).

Nxai Pan is covered with short, sweet grasses and islands of umbrella thorn (*Vachellia tortilis*) bushes. Unlike the salt pans, this pan is richly vegetated because its saline-free clay soils provide a more fertile environment

Clumps of umbrella thorn bushes, almost leafless during the dry season, grow on Nxai Pan.

Baines' Baobabs are almost unchanged since Thomas Baines painted them in 1862. Today they are a national monument.

Two impala rams spar at Nxai Pan. Only occasionally, usually during the rut, will sparring escalate into a fight.

for root growth. Species growing on calcrete soils around the pan include trumpet thorn (*Catophractes alexandri*) and purplepod clusterleaf (*Terminalia prunioides*).

Along the eastern margin of Kudiakam Pan is a cluster of massive baobabs (*Adansonia digitata*), collectively known as Baines' Baobabs. This group of large trees is alternatively called the 'Sleeping Sisters' or the 'Seven Sisters'. Today a national monument, Baines' Baobabs were named after the explorer, naturalist and painter, Thomas Baines, who painted them in 1862.

## Wildlife

The northern section, and particularly Nxai Pan, is a haven for wildlife. Grazers that are well adapted to the dry Kalahari bush savanna are drawn by the sweet grasses that proliferate here. In years of good rainfall, large herds of impala and springbok, together with their newborn calves, graze on the pans, a rare occurrence, as they normally occupy separate habitats. In fact, this is one of the few places in southern Africa where visitors can see the two species together; the only other place where this occurs is around Etosha Pan in Namibia.

Thousands of zebra and blue wildebeest migrate from their dry range along the Boteti River to the Nxai Pan area after the rains. Hartebeest, the drought-adapted gemsbok and even buffalo also congregate in significant numbers on the pan at this time, taking advantage of good grazing opportunities, while greater kudu prefer the stands of mopane trees that surround the pan. Giraffe, attracted to the tiny, fresh leaves of

A thirsty giraffe enjoys a sip or two of fresh water at Nxai Pan.

Water and nutritious grasses draw herds of elephants and zebra to the plains of the Makgadikgadi and Nxai Pans National Park.

acacia trees, and elephants, seen around the permanent water source on the pan, are other large mammals for which to look out.

Predators such as brown and spotted hyenas, lions, cheetahs and African wild dogs find easy prey among the antelope and their young.

Lionesses slake their thirst at a water hole.

Black-backed jackal, honey badgers and bat-eared fox also occur throughout the area.

The southern section of the park encompasses both Kalahari and riverine habitats. Towards the west, the Boteti River is where large herds of zebra and blue wildebeest, accompanied by gemsbok, eland and red hartebeest, range during the dry winter months. The woodlands along the river banks shelter bushbuck, impala, duiker and greater kudu, and large permanent water pools along the Boteti are home to hippo. This section of the park also draws a healthy population of predators. The big cats – leopards, cheetah and lions – are well represented, while spotted and brown hyenas occasionally roam the area.

Impala often gather around Khumaga Camp, which overlooks the Boteti. Troops of baboons and vervet monkeys forage here too. Also near the camp is Hippo Pool, where a pod of hippos has taken up permanent residence.

Towards the southeast, herds of springbok range along the fringes of Ntwetwe Pan, and

A lone black-backed jackal and a wake of vultures compete for tasty morsels at a zebra kill.

steenbok commonly browse on woody plants. Predators occuring in the vicinity of Ntwetwe Pan include lions, brown hyenas, black-backed jackal and bat-eared foxes.

## Birdlife

Bird lovers should head to the Boteti River, where a wide variety of riverine and bush birds can be observed. African fish eagles, hornbills, grey go-away-birds, southern white-crowned shrikes and glossy starlings occupy the trees, while red-billed spurfowl and helmeted guineafowl can be seen scampering through the undergrowth. Watch out for pairs of double-banded sandgrouse when driving near the river; they have a habit of flying down and landing on the ground in front of your vehicle before taking off again.

Further away from the river, birds are generally scarce. Sightings of ostriches are guaranteed almost all year round. Depending on rainfall, visitors may be lucky enough to see the chicks trailing after their parents along the tracks.

Summer is a good time for seeing birds of prey. Waterbirds, too, are abundant at this time of year, gathering at temporary pans after the rains.

Helmeted guineafowl forage for food.

113

# Things to do

## Guided drives

The national park does not offer tours (or any other activities) for visitors. However, Gweta Lodge and Planet Baobab run full-day trips to Nxai Pan; Gweta Lodge runs full-day trips to the Boteti River; and Boteti River Camp in Khumaga village offers game drives into the park. Kwando Safaris, operators of Nxai Pan Camp, have a range of highly experienced guides and dedicated trackers who take guests on game drives in the Nxai Pan section of the national park.

Jack's Camp, San Camp and Camp Kalahari take guests on game drives and night drives in their custom-built 4x4s to see the desert wildlife.

## Self-guided drives

Drives along the Boteti River are particularly rewarding, especially the route northwards from Khumaga Camp to the hippo pools. In the north, the track that encircles Nxai Pan affords some great opportunities for viewing wildlife.

Note that some tracks are for staff only, and access is not allowed for visitors. It is also

Elephants are some of the animals that can be seen on a guided tour of Nxai Pan with Kwando Safaris.

difficult to observe the zebra and wildebeest herds around Ntwetwe Pan in summer – there are very few tracks and the area is subject to flooding at this time.

## Horse riding

Horseback safaris are available for guests at Jack's Camp, San Camp and Camp Kalahari. These are usually two hours long, but more experienced riders can sign up for multiday riding safaris.

Tailored to all levels of experience, the horseback safaris at Jack's Camp and San Camp allow guests to view wildlife at close quarters.

UNCHARTED AFRICA/NATURAL SELECTION

Guides at Jack's Camp give guests a glimpse of the San's traditional hunting methods, of which digging for scorpions is one.

### Walks with San trackers

Guests at Nxai Pan Camp, Jack's Camp, San Camp and Camp Kalahari can enjoy an informative guided walk with a trained San tracker. On the walks the guides share their knowledge about the nomadic lifestyle of the San and the changing culture of this community. Subjects covered include traditional hunting methods and the gathering of plants (and their medicinal uses). There are also demonstrations of how to make a fire and how to use a digging stick.

### Quad-bike safari

For the adventure-loving traveller, Jack's Camp, San Camp and Camp Kalahari offer a five-night quad-biking expedition across Ntwetwe Pan to Lekhubu Island and back. Accommodation on the first and last nights is at any one of the three establishments, while the rest of the time is spent on the rocky island. This activity takes place only during the dry season, when the surface of the pan is at its hardest.

## Places to stay

The park and two of its camps are managed by Botswana's Department of Wildlife and National Parks (DWNP), while the rest of the camps are run by private operators.

It is best to reserve your accommodation well ahead of your visit. Bookings for the camps managed by DWNP may also be made at the department's Maun office. Visitors who turn up without a prior booking may rent a stand, if one is available. Those wishing to stay at the DWNP camps may pay at the entrance gates, but payments must be made in cash, as credit card facilities are not available. Those without bookings for the privately run camps may also pay on arrival at those camps.

A selection of privately managed bush lodges and tented camps can be found on the outskirts of the park.

### South Camp

This camp site, operated by the Xomae Group, is located amid mopane woodland on the southern edge of Nxai Pan. The camping ground consists of 10 stands, two ablution blocks, standpipes and an artificial water hole.

### Khumaga Camp

Khumaga Camp, operated by the Savuti Khwai Linyanti group of camps, is 2 kilometres north of the Khumaga entrance gate. Its location, overlooking the Boteti River, makes it an ideal base for exploring the riverine woodlands and surrounds. To reach the camp, you will need to cross the river by means of a pontoon ferry.

The camp site offers 10 spacious stands shaded by large camel thorn trees and solar-powered ablution blocks that include toilets and showers. Note that the water is not suitable for drinking.

Visitors who turn up without a prior booking may rent a stand if available. Payments at the camp must be made in cash, as there are no credit card facilities.

The luxury Nxai Pan Camp is located on the western edge of the fossil pan.

### Nxai Pan Camp

Run by Kwando Safaris, the luxurious Nxai Pan Camp has nine en-suite tents overlooking a water hole. The camp, located along the western edge of Nxai Pan, also includes an open-air lounge and dining space, a bar, a swimming pool and a curio shop.

### Tree Island Camp

Tree Island Camp, on the eastern plains near Ntwetwe Pan, is managed by the DWNP. The only facilities here are pit latrines and bucket showers. Visitors must bring their own water.

### Baines' Baobabs Camp

At Baines' Baobabs Camp, on the eastern shore of Kudiakam Pan, are three stands, all shaded by these massive trees. The camp is managed by the Xomae Group.

### Njuca Hills Camp

Operated by the DWNP, Njuca Hills Camp lies on low-lying sand dunes in the south of the park, providing expansive views across the surrounding grasslands. Facilities include pit latrines and bucket showers. Campers must bring their own water.

### Jack's Camp, San Camp and Camp Kalahari

Run by Natural Selection, Jack's Camp, San Camp and Camp Kalahari are three small, fun, quirky camps that operate in a 450,000-hectare private reserve abutting the eastern boundary of the national park. Although the camps vary in design, size and price, guests enjoy the same range of activities.

The Bedouin-themed Jack's Camp offers 10 luxurious tents, each furnished with an eclectic array of collectables and artefacts accumulated by the owners over many decades. Persian carpets, muslin-draped walls, velvet-covered chairs and colourful textiles complete the décor, making a stay at this camp truly exceptional. Tents are a signature feature here, with meals, tea and drinks all served under a canvas canopy. Even the swimming pool has its own tent.

The elegant tents of San Camp line the shore of Ntwetwe Pan, the white canvas quarters evoking a sense of romanticism amid the vastness of the ancient salt-encrusted lake.

Shaded by tall palm trees, the tented homes at Jack's Camp are a combination of luxury, style and comfort.

In keeping with a more minimalist style, the seven tents are equipped with comfortable four-poster beds, elegant armchairs and Persian rugs, and all have en-suite bathrooms and indoor showers. Meals are served in a mess tent.

Set among acacia trees and stands of tall palms, Camp Kalahari is Natural Selection's most affordable offering. Eleven canvas tents, including en-suite bathrooms, cater for couples, families and larger groups. Common spaces include a large living and dining area, a library and a swimming pool.

## Getting there

Access to the park is through five entrance gates: Nxai Pan is the gateway to the northern section of the sanctuary, while Makolwane, Xire Xare, Phuduhudu and Khumaga provide access to the park's southern section. Opening times are 6am–6.30pm during winter and 5.30am–7pm during summer. Maps and copies of the park's rules and regulations are usually available at the gates. Up-to-date information can also be obtained from the game scout camp at Nxai Pan itself.

■ **Nxai Pan gate:** This gate is 64 kilometres west of the Gweta turnoff along the Nata–Maun road.

■ **Makolwane gate:** This gate can be reached from the Nata–Maun road. Approaching from Nata, continue westwards after the turnoff to Gweta. After about 12 kilometres, you will see a gravel track running parallel to the main road. Follow this track for 3 kilometres until you reach the entrance gate.

■ **Xire Xare gate:** This gate lies 24 kilometres south of Makolwane gate. Note that the initial entrance is via Makolwane, and entrance and camping fees must be paid here before proceeding to Xire Xare. From Makolwane, follow a sandy track to Xire Xare.

■ **Phuduhudu gate:** This gate is 75 kilometres west of the Gweta turnoff along the Nata–Maun road and 11 kilometres westwards from Nxai Pan gate along the same road.

■ **Khumaga gate:** This gate provides entry from the southwest, and can be reached via Khumaga, a small village along the Letlhakane–Maun road. Turn off the main road and pass through the village until you reach the Boteti River. The gate is on the other side of the river. There is normally no problem crossing the river by vehicle, since it is usually dry. However, in recent years, the river has begun to flow again and visitors must use a ferry to cross the water.

When the Boteti is in flow, visitors heading for the park's Khumaga gate have to be ferried across the river.

# Practical information for visitors

## CHAPTER 11

The Makgadikgadi Pans have over the last few years been gaining popularity as a tourism destination, and nowadays travellers are likely to spend several days exploring the region.

Although fairly remote, the pans can be reached by means of a good network of roads from any point of entry to the country – whether from a border post or from the capital Gaborone. Other facilities and services in the region range from modest to upmarket. Accommodation in lodges, inns and camp sites is available in and around most towns and villages, and most of these are equipped with the basics. Restaurants and other places to eat can be found in some of the larger towns, but are non-existent in the smaller villages. Travellers are thus advised to stock up on food and other necessities in places such as Gaborone or Francistown.

Most places have medical facilities, in case of an emergency, and there are police stations in the bigger centres. There is a good communications system, although network coverage does not extend to all parts of the Makgadikgadi. The provision of Wi-Fi access is limited to a few lodges or internet cafés along the way.

The tourist season lasts all year round (see Chapter 3), but autumn and winter, which bring lower temperatures, are popular times.

This brief travel advisory covers all the basics first-time and repeat travellers to the country and the Makgadikgadi Pans, in particular, need to know.

## Getting there

### By air

There are regular daily flights between Johannesburg and Gaborone, operated by Air Botswana and several South African carriers. Air Namibia runs daily flights to Gaborone from Durban. The Johannesburg–Francistown route is served three times a week by Air Botswana – on Mondays, Tuesdays and Thursdays. There are also daily flights between Gaborone and Francistown, operated by Air Botswana.

For travellers wishing to start their journey in Maun, Air Botswana offers four flights a week between Johannesburg and Maun.

An off-road vehicle is necessary to navigate the Makgadikgadi region's sandy tracks, such as this one leading through dense grass to Sowa Pan.

## By road

Tarred roads link Botswana to all her neighbours – South Africa, Zimbabwe, Namibia and Zambia. These roads are suitable for ordinary motor vehicles but the surface may be corrugated or in need of repair in places.

■ **Intercape** runs daily services between Johannesburg and Gaborone. Buses leave Johannesburg at noon, arriving in Gaborone at 7.30pm. For further information and bookings, call (0027) 21 3804400 or (00267) 3974294.

■ **Khanda Express** operates a direct service between Johannesburg and Francistown four times a week – on Sundays, Mondays, Wednesdays and Fridays. Buses leave Johannesburg at 12.30pm, arriving in Francistown at 10pm. For further information and bookings, call (00267) 2416471.

■ **AT&T Monnakgotla** operates daily services between Johannesburg and Gaborone. Buses leave Johannesburg at 3pm, arriving in Gaborone at 8pm. For further information and bookings, call (0027) 786443839 or (00267) 3995900 / 71375722.

## Guidelines for driving in the Makgadikgadi Pans region

A reliable four-wheel drive vehicle is essential for visiting many of the places mentioned in this book, especially the pans and the margins around them.

Avoid driving on the pans at all costs during the wet season. Watch out for dark patches on the pans during the dry season; such areas will be wet below the surface.

Only drive on the pans when the surface is completely dry, and then only follow well-marked tracks indicating that other vehicles have passed by recently.

Do not drive at night, even on the tarred main roads. Roads and tracks are usually unfenced and livestock, as well as wild animals, are likely to wander across them during both the day and night.

Ideally, two or more vehicles should travel together in case one of the vehicles breaks down or there is a medical emergency. A satellite phone may come in handy.

It is easy to get lost on the pans or in remote areas. Ensure that you have a reliable GPS.

Seeds from tall grasses growing along the middle ridge of some tracks may block your radiator. This can cause an increase in water temperature, resulting in your engine overheating. To avoid this problem, attach a piece of shade netting in front of the radiator. Also, constantly check your water temperature gauge.

Regularly check below the vehicle in case grass has collected there. If it is not removed, the grass might catch fire, especially if it is in contact with the exhaust pipe.

Watch out for places like this on the pans – the firm pan surface hides from view the waterlogged saline clay below.

# Tourist information

Botswana Tourism has an office in the Fairgrounds Office Park in Gaborone. The office park is located on the left side of the road from the Tlokweng Gate border post.
Fairscape Precinct Building
Fairgrounds Office Park
Gaborone
**Tel:** (00267) 3913111
**Email:** marketing@botswanatourism.co.bw
**Website:** www.botswanatourism.co.bw

# Travelling within Botswana

You can reach the pans on good tarred roads, suitable for saloon cars, from Gaborone and Francistown. To reach Francistown from Gaborone (a distance of 440 kilometres), take the A1 road. From Francistown, there is a choice of two routes to the pans: the A30 road runs westwards to Orapa and Letlhakane, allowing access to the southern margins of the pans, while the A3 road takes you in a northwesterly direction to Nata and Gweta, providing access to the northern margins of the pans. However, take care between Nata and Gweta – here the road has potholes and there may still be diversions, a result of widespread flooding during the 2016/17 and 2017/18 rainy seasons.

If you enter Botswana at the Martin's Drift/Groblersbrug border post, you can take the B140 road westwards to Palapye. From here, take the A1 road to Francistown and then follow the routes outlined above to the pans. You can also take the A14 northwestwards from Palapye to Letlhakane.

However, to fully explore the pans area away from the tarred roads, a 4x4 or 2x4 pickup truck is essential. Such vehicles will allow access to routes to Lekhubu Island, across the pans, along the Mosu/Kaitshe Escarpment and in the Makgadikgadi and Nxai Pans National Park (only 4x4 vehicles are allowed to enter the park).

# Buses

Buses are a convenient way of getting from Gaborone to the main centres around the Makgadikgadi Pans. Buses from Gaborone to Francistown leave every 30 minutes during the day and the journey takes about five hours. Some buses also run between Gaborone and Letlhakane/Orapa and a one-way journey takes about six hours. Buses leaving from Francistown for Maun via Nata and Gweta take between two and two-and-a-half hours to reach Nata and four hours to get to Gweta.

# Car hire

There are several car rental agencies in Botswana and tariffs vary according to the type of vehicle being hired.

The following companies have offices in both Gaborone and Francistown:
- **Avis: Tel:** (00267) 3913093 (Gaborone) / 2413901 (Francistown)
  **Email:** botswana.reservations@avisbudget.co.za
  **Website:** www.avis.co.za
- **Bidvest Car Rental:**
  **Tel:** (00267) 3903477 (Gaborone) / 2440083 or 71223838 (Francistown)
  **Email:** gbkiosk@bcr.co.za
  **Website:** www.bidvestcarrental.co.za
- **Europcar: Tel:** (00267) 3902280 (Gaborone) / 2404282 (Francistown)
  **Email:** ona.masaka@europcar.co.za
  **Website:** www.europcar.co.za

# Fuel

Towns and villages en route to the Makgadikgadi Pans have service stations, but bear in mind that the distances between them can be considerable. For example, there are no service stations between Serowe and Letlhakane – a distance of some 200 kilometres. Also, some of the more remote filling stations in small villages may occasionally run out of fuel. So fill up whenever you can.

Filling stations operate in Serowe, Mokubilo, Letlhakane, Mopipi, Rakops, Francistown, Sebina, Dukwi, Nata and Gweta. Most service stations sell regular lead replacement fuel as well as unleaded fuel and diesel. Some filling stations have small convenience stores that sell foodstuffs, cold drinks and toiletries.

Credit cards are accepted, but keep enough cash in case the system is out of operation.

### Vehicle-repair facilities

Many service garages in Francistown and Letlhakane carry out vehicle repairs. Details of similar facilities throughout the region are mentioned in Chapter 6 and in the list of contact details (see p. 127). Informal 'bush mechanics' may be found almost anywhere and most do not keep to strict opening hours.

### Traffic rules

The speed limit on open roads is 120 kilometres per hour, whereas in towns and villages it is 60 kilometres per hour. Speeding fines depend on the speed of the vehicle at the time. For other infringements, fines can be steep.

Wearing seat belts is obligatory and you must always carry your driver's license with you (photocopies are *not acceptable*).

## Entry requirements

All travellers should be in possession of a passport valid for at least six months. No visas are required for South Africans for stays of up to 90 days.

## Botswana–South Africa border posts

The following two border posts are most convenient for visitors coming from South Africa:

### Tlokweng Gate/Kopfontein

This is the busiest border crossing between Botswana and South Africa. It is located on the road between Zeerust and Gaborone, the closest centres on both sides of the border.
**Opening hours:** 6am–12 midnight
**Tel:** (00267) 3105409

### Martin's Drift/Groblersbrug

This border post is located along the Limpopo River on the road between Mokopane and Palapye. It is a very quiet border crossing and formalities usually take less than 15 minutes. However, it can be very busy during holiday periods, especially at Christmas and Easter. On rare occasions, the border may be closed in the event of severe flooding along the Limpopo River.
**Opening hours:** 6am–10pm
**Tel:** (00267) 4940254

## Customs

Visitors are allowed to bring up to 20 kilograms each of fresh beef, goat and pork meat across the border, except during outbreaks of livestock diseases when meat imports are strictly forbidden.

There are a number of veterinary checkpoints inside the country, and permits may be required to pass through some of these checkpoints with fresh meat. No permits are required for tinned meat products.

Visitors are not allowed to bring fresh fruit across the border.

## Emergencies
### Useful numbers
- **Emergency Assist:** 991 / (00267) 3904537
- **Med Rescue:** 992
- **Rescue One:** 993
- **Ambulance:** 997
- **Fire Brigade:** 998
- **Police:** 999

### South African High Commission
South African citizens who encounter serious trouble may contact the South African High

Commission in Gaborone at: South African High Commission (located in Main Mall)
Plot 29, Queens Road
**Tel:** (00267) 3904800 / 1 / 2 / 3
**Fax:** (00267) 3905502
**Email:** sahcgabs@btc.mail.co.bw

## Police

There are police stations in Letlhakane, Gweta and Nata (see pp. 127, 128 and 129 for contact details). The police must always be contacted when accidents occur. If you have vehicle insurance, the police will prepare an accident report for your insurance company.

## Money and banks

Botswana's currency is the pula, with one pula equal to 100 thebe. The word *pula* means 'rain' in Setswana. Notes come in denominations of P10, P20, P50, P100 and differ in colour and size. There are coins of 5, 10, 25 and 50 thebe and 1, 2 and 5 pula.

In recent years, the pula has strengthened against the rand; at the time of writing, the exchange rate was about P1 = R1.30.

The major Botswana banks – First National Bank of Botswana, Barclays Botswana and Standard Chartered Bank Botswana – offer the full range of banking services and ATMs in Letlhakane and Francistown. There is also a small Barclays branch, with an ATM, in Nata.

Credit cards are generally accepted, especially in most upmarket lodges and at filling stations, but facilities are unreliable in remote areas, and it is recommended that you have cash on hand in case of an emergency.

## Public holidays

Government offices, banks and most large businesses close during public holidays. Border posts remain open during these days, and public transport continues as normal. Smaller enterprises, hotels, museums and national parks also stay open.

- **January 1:** New Year's Day
- **January 2:** Public holiday
- **March/April:** Easter and Good Friday – these dates vary from year to year.
- **May 1:** Labour Day
- **May:** Ascension Day – this day falls on the Thursday 40 days after Easter Sunday.
- **July 1:** Sir Seretse Khama Day
- **July:** President's Day – this day usually falls on the third Monday in July, with the following day also observed as a public holiday.
- **September 30:** Botswana Day
- **October 1:** Botswana Day
- **December 25:** Christmas Day
- **December 26:** Boxing Day

If a public holiday falls on a Sunday, the following Monday is observed as a public holiday.

## Time

Like South Africa, Botswana is two hours ahead of GMT throughout the year.

## Communication
### Telephones

The international dialling code for Botswana is 00267. Botswana does not use area codes. To phone someone in Botswana, follow the international dialling code with the person's landline number.

Botswana's landline telephone system is operated by Botswana Telecommunications Corporation (BTC).

### Cellphones

Mobile phones are widely used in Botswana. The main cellphone operators are Mascom Wireless, Orange Botswana and BeMobile – the latter has the best network coverage around the pans. However, the more remote areas may have no coverage at all and a satellite phone may be useful in such places.

It is relatively easy to obtain a local SIM card, even in small places such as Nata. Prepaid cards can be bought in many places, including supermarkets and filling station convenience stores.

## Postal services

There are post offices in Letlhakane, Sowa Town, Mopipi, Gweta and Nata. Opening hours are Monday–Friday (8am–4pm) and Saturday (8.30am–12 noon). They provide the usual services, including money transfers.

## Health precautions

### Tetanus, hepatitis, typhoid and malaria

Although no vaccinations are required for visitors entering Botswana, it is wise to be vaccinated against tetanus, hepatitis and typhoid. However, the greatest health threat comes from malaria, caused by a parasite transmitted to humans by the *Anopheles* mosquito, especially during the rainy season when areas of standing water provide ideal places for these insects to breed. The Makgadikgadi Pans area is a malaria area and you are strongly advised to consult a doctor about anti-malarial medication before you set out on your trip.

### Rabies

Do not allow dogs to approach you – although rabies is now rare in Botswana, it is better to be safe than sorry. Remember that in remote rural areas, jackals are carriers of the disease and can easily pass it on to domestic dogs. If you are bitten, seek medical attention immediately. Clinics here will start you on a course of anti-rabies vaccinations.

### Water

Tap water is usually safe to drink, but may sometimes be a little salty. Some travellers prefer to bring their own fresh water with them. Bottled mineral water is locally available.

### Sunburn

Do not underestimate the damage the sun can cause, especially during the hot summer months. Protect yourself with sun lotion, wear a hat, and drink plenty of water.

### Dust

During the dry season, the pans are very dusty, especially when the wind blows. Avoid being out on the pans during this time of the year if you are asthmatic. The dust may also irritate sensitive eyes.

### Medical care

Should you require medical attention, there are government primary hospitals in Letlhakane and Gweta and government clinics in most of the larger villages in the area. Ambulances are usually available to transport patients to a hospital, if required. Note that health posts in smaller villages provide only basic services.

Private medical practitioners, who offer a quicker and more personal service to patients, can be found in Letlhakane, Nata and Sowa Town.

The only pharmacies in the region are found in Francistown and Letlhakane.

## Travellers with disabilities

Very few establishments are equipped for disabled visitors.

## Eating and drinking

There are very few places to eat out in the region, with Francistown and Letlhakane being the only towns that have a range of restaurants from which to choose. Closer to Sowa Pan, Nata village has one restaurant. Takeaways, usually at convenience stores at filling stations, are available in Nata and Gweta. Some lodges will also cater for non-residents. See pp. 127–134 for contact details of lodges and inns in the region.

If you are not staying in a lodge or an inn that provides meals, you would need to purchase your food before setting off for the pans. With the exception of Nata, villages in the area do not have well-stocked supermarkets. Although there are general dealers in these places, they sell only basic foodstuffs and a few toiletries.

Smaller villages have tuck shops, usually a small room or a shed in someone's compound, where a limited range of goods can be bought.

## Accommodation

Places to stay at range from basic camp sites to bed and breakfast establishments, guest houses and upmarket lodges and safari camps. Details of accommodation options in the Makgadikgadi region are given in Chapters 6–10. For reservations, see pp. 127–134 for contact details.

Depending on the place and season, rates may vary from about P400–P500 per night to more than P1,000 for a room at an upmarket lodge.

## Reservations at the Makgadikgadi and Nxai Pans National Park

The Makgadikgadi and Nxai Pans National Park is managed by Botswana's Department of Wildlife and National Parks (DWNP). Two of the camp sites in the park are managed by the DWNP, with the rest run by private operators.

It is advisable to book, and pay, in advance to secure a camp site. Payment can be made at DWNP offices in pulas or rands, or by credit card.

Note that the DWNP office in Maun manages the bookings of camp sites in the parks and reserves of northern Botswana (Makgadikgadi and Nxai Pans National Park, Chobe National Park and Moremi Game Reserve). Once you have made your booking, you will receive a booking number to give to an officer at the entrance gate of the park or reserve where you have chosen to stay.

Visitors arriving at any of the parks or reserves without a prior reservation will be allowed to enter as long as a camp site is available. In such cases, payment must be made in cash.

**To book any of the DWNP-managed camp sites, contact:**
Parks and Reserves Reservations Office (Gaborone)
**Tel:** (00267) 3180774 / 3996543
**Fax:** (00267) 3180775
**Email:** dwnp@gov.bw
Bookings may also be made at the DWNP office in Maun and payment made at the gates:
**Tel:** (00267) 6861265 / 6860368

To book any of the camp sites managed by private operators – Xomae Group, Kwando Safaris or Savuti Khwai Linyanti (SKL) Group of Camps – see p. 133 for contact details.

Khumaga entrance gate, Makgadikgadi and Nxai Pans National Park.

# Contact details

## CHAPTER 12

Useful contact details for places to stay, adventure companies, event organizers and parks and reserves listed in Chapters 6–10 are given below. In addition, contact information is also provided for key services and facilities available in the bigger towns and villages that may be of use to travellers.

## TOWNS AND VILLAGES
(see pp. 56–75)

### Gweta

#### Places to stay

**Planet Baobab**
Tel: (0027) 11 3264407; Cell: (00267) 72338344
Email: res@planetbaobab.travel
Website: www.naturalselection.travel

**Gweta Lodge**
Tel: (00267) 6212220
Cell: (00267) 73444006 / 73562689
Email: gwetalodge@btcmail.co.bw
Website: www.gwetalodge.co.za

**Chaixara Backpackers**
Cell: (00267) 75352134 (reservations) / 73682528
Email: chaixaracamp2017@gmail.com

#### Facilities and services
**Police station:** Tel: (00267) 6212222
**Government primary hospital:** Tel: (00267) 6212333

#### Vehicle- and puncture-repair services
- **Gweta Brigades:** Servicing, basic repairs, puncture repairs; open Monday–Friday 7.30am–4.30pm. Tel: (00267) 6212214

#### Things to do
For activities listed on p. 67, contact Planet Baobab and Gweta Lodge. See 'Places to stay' (above) for the relevant contact details.

The sun paints the sky in shades of red, orange and yellow as it sets over a flooded Sowa Pan.

Quad biking on Ntwetwe Pan.

# Nata

## Places to stay

**Northgate Lodge**
Tel: (00267) 6211156/55
Cell: (00267) 73953607
Fax: (00267) 6211154
Email: nglreceptionnata@gmail.com
Website: www.northgatelodge.com

**Maya Lodge**
Tel: (00267) 6211296; Fax: (00267) 6211005
Cell: (00267) 75554378
Email: chrysalis26bw@gmail.com

**Nata Guest Inn**
Tel: (00267) 6211334 / 75485108
Cell: (00267) 71756142
Email: gabomorewanare@gmail.com

**Gomwe Guest Inn**
Tel: (00267) 2470725 / 71736446
Email: gomweguestinn@gmail.com

**Nata Lodge**
Tel: (00267) 2471112
Email: reservations@natalodge.com
Website: www.natalodge.com

**Pelican Lodge and Camping**
Tel: (00267) 2470117
Fax: (00267) 2470170
Email: reservations@pelicanlodge.co.bw /
banqueting@pelicanlodge.co.bw

**Elephant Sands Bush Lodge & Campsite**
Cell: (00267) 73445162
Email: bookings@elephantsandsbotswana.com
Website: www.elephantsands.com

**Dzibanana Lodge and Camping**
Tel: (00267) 2470117 / 2470808
Cell: (00267) 73644444 / 73417113
Email: generalmanager@thewildlodges.com
Website: www.thewildlodges.com

## Facilities and services

Police station: Tel: (00267) 6211118

**Medical services**
- Government clinic: Tel: (00267) 6211244
- Proland Medical Centre: Private facility.
  Tel: (00267) 6211243
  Cell: (00267) 71771765
  (after hours/emergency)

**Filling stations**
There are three filling stations, all with
convenience stores; open 24 hours.

**Vehicle- and puncture-repair services**
- Imper Spares: Servicing, basic repairs,
  engine overhauls, towing service; open daily.
  Cell: (00267) 72198589 / 75417703
- JJ Engineering: Servicing, basic repairs,
  puncture repairs, 24-hour breakdown/
  towing service; open daily except Saturdays.
  Tel: (00267) 6211363

- **Phillip Welding: Cell:** (00267) 72410138
- **Trinquar Tyre Services:** Puncture repairs, wheel balancing, new and second-hand tyres for sale; open daily. **Cell:** (00267) 71671078

## Things to do

For activities listed on pp. 67 and 68, contact Nata, Pelican and Northgate lodges and Elephant Sands Bush Lodge & Campsite. See 'Places to stay' (p. 128) for the relevant contact details.

## Sowa Town
### Places to stay
**Makgadikgadi Lodge**
**Cell:** (00267) 74001884
**Email:** makgadikgadi@boitekanelo.ac.bw

### Facilities and services
**Police station: Tel:** (00267) 6213222

### Medical services
- **Government clinic: Tel:** (00267) 6213199
- **Tati River Clinic:** Private facility. **Tel:** (00267) 6213008; **Cell:** (00267) 75752703 / 76556147 (after hours/emergency)

### Things to do
**Skydiving (Makgadikgadi Epic)**
Botswana Tourism Organisation
**Tel:** (00267) 3913111

**Race for Rhinos**
Botswana Tourism Organisation
**Tel:** (00267) 3913111

**Makgadikgadi Country Club**
**Cell:** (00267) 74001884

## Letlhakane
### Places to stay
**Mikelele Motel**
**Tel:** (00267) 2978594 / 2976639
**Fax:** (00267) 2976268

**Email:** reception.mikelele@gmail.com / morwadi.tape@gmail.com

**Makumutu Lodge and Campsite**
**Tel:** (00267) 2960203/4/5
**Email:** reservations@makumutusafarilodge.com / makumutulodge@gmail.com
**Website:** www.makumutusafarilodge.com

**Tuuthebe Lodge and Campsite**
**Cell:** (00267) 72121913
**Email:** info@tuuthebe.com
**Website:** www.tuuthebe.com

### Facilities and services
**Police station: Tel:** (00267) 2978222

### Medical services
- **Government primary hospital: Tel:** (00267) 2978242
- **Karibu Medical Centre:** Private facility. **Tel:** (00267) 2974540
- **Rapha Medical Centre:** Private facility. **Tel:** (00267) 2976003
- **St Damian Medical Clinic:** Private facility. **Tel:** (00267) 2976072

### Vehicle- and puncture-repair services
- **Tyre World:** Puncture repairs **Tel:** (00267) 29764473
- **Motovac:** Motor spares. **Tel:** (00267) 2976655

## Orapa
Orapa is a private mining town and visitors must obtain a permit to enter the town. Permits can be obtained from the Debswana mining company in Orapa or from Makumutu Lodge and Campsite (guests only), between Letlhakane and Orapa.
- **Debswana: Tel:** (00267) 2902000
- **Makumutu Lodge and Campsite: Tel:** (00267) 2960203/4/5

Meno a Kwena Camp.

## Mopipi
### Facilities and services
**Filling stations**
There are two fillings stations, Cooperative filling station and Mopipi filling station, both of which are open from 6am–10pm. Mopipi filling station also has a convenience store.

## Rakops
### Places to stay
**Xere Motel**
**Tel:** (00267) 2975068; **Cell:** (00267) 72675568
**Email:** info@xeremotelrakops.com

**Rakops River Lodge**
**Tel:** (00267) 3932711; **Cell:** (00267) 71434129
**Email:** bookings@rakopsriverlodge.com / omokopi@rakopsriverlodge.com
**Website:** www.rakopsriverlodge.com

**Matsaudi Camp Site**
**Cell:** (00267) 74304924
**Email:** rockylekanyang@yahoo.com

### Facilities and services
**Police: Tel:** (00267) 2975115 / 2975128
**Government hospital: Tel:** (00267) 2975111

**Vehicle and puncture repairs**
- **Isago Wheel and Tyre:** Puncture repairs, servicing, welding, wheel balancing, basic motor spares and tyres for sale.
  **Tel:** (00267) 75685078

- **Rakops Spare and Tyre Service:** Puncture repairs only; open daily.
  **Tel:** (00267) 73945951 / 72484134

### Things to do
For activities listed on p. 75, contact Rakops River Lodge. See 'Places to stay' (this page) for the relevant contact details.

## Khumaga
### Places to stay
**Meno a Kwena Camp**
**Tel:** (0027) 11 3264407
**Email:** reservations@naturalselection.travel
**Website:** www.naturalselection.travel

**Leroo La Tau**
**Tel:** (0027) 11 3943873; (00267) 6861243 / 6861559 / 6862246
**Email:** info@desertdelta.com
**Website:** www.desertdelta.com

**Boteti River Camp (formerly Tiaan's Camp)**
**Tel:** (00267) 6863685
**Cell:** (00267) 77152753 / 72234998
**Email:** botetirivercamp@bushways.com
**Website:** www.botetirivercamp.com

### Things to do
For activities listed on p. 75, contact Meno a Kwena Camp, Leroo La Tau and Boteti River Camp. See 'Places to stay' (above) for the relevant contact details.

# MOSU/KAITSHE ESCARPMENT
(see pp. 76–85)

## Facilities and services

**Government health post (Mosu):**
Tel: (00267) 2910217

**Filling station (Mokubilo)**
One filling station; open daily from 8am–8pm.
Cell: (00267) 73840546

**Vehicle and puncture repairs (Mosu)**
■ Ngontotini Puncture Repair and Welding:
   Cell: (00267) 76251576

## Places to stay

**Moriti wa Selemo Adventures Bush Camp**
Cell: (00267) 73777428 (reservations) / (00267)
75804199 (trips) / 2970595
Email: andriesinmoriti@gmail.com

## Things to do

**Off-road biking, cycling and quad biking**
■ Muddy Face Botswana:
   Cell: (00267) 71216904
   Email: lola@muddyfacebotswana.co.bw
   Website: www.muddyfacebotswana.co.bw

Mea Pan.

**Guided drives and walks, quad biking and land yachting**
■ Moriti wa Selemo Adventures:
   Cell: (00267) 73777428 (reservations) /
   (00267) 75804199 (trips)
   Email: andriesinmoriti@gmail.com

# LEKHUBU ISLAND
(see pp. 86–97)

## Places to stay

**Lekhubu Island Camp Site**
Reservations and payment: Gaing O Community
Trust
Tel/fax: (00267) 2979612
Cell: (00267) 75494669 / 73109996
Email: kubu.island@btcmail.co.bw
Website: www.kubuisland.com

**Makgadikgadi Adventure Camp**
Cell: (00267) 74453703 (reservations) /
74531017 (information)
Email: info@makgadikgadiadventurecamp.co.bw
Website: www.makgadikgadiadventurecamp.
co.bw

## Things to do

**Guided hikes**
■ Gaing O Community Trust:
   Tel/fax: (00267) 2979612
   Cell: (00267) 75494669 / 73109996
   Email: kubu.island@btcmail.co.bw
   Website: www.kubuisland.com

**Charity hikes**
■ YCare Charitable Trust:
   Tel: (00267) 3932253
   Cell: (00267) 71784212
   Email: info@ycare.org.bw
   Website: www.ycare.org.bw

**Guided 4x4 tours**
Contact Gweta Lodge. See 'Places to stay' on
p. 127 for the relevant contact details.

Nata Bird Sanctuary, Sowa Pan..

## NATA BIRD SANCTUARY
(see pp. 98–105)

### Places to stay
**Nata Bird Sanctuary Camp Site**
**Cell:** (00267) 71544342
**Email:** nataconservationtrust@gmail.com
**Website:** www.natasanctuary.org.bw
For accommodation options outside Nata Bird Sanctuary, see the listing of establishments in and around Nata village on p. 128.

### Things to do
**Sunset trips**
Contact Nata, Pelican and Northgate lodges. See 'Places to stay' on p. 128 for the relevant contact details.

### Quad biking
- ATV Adventurer:
  **Cell:** (00267) 73376493 / 72886403
  **Email:** info@atvadventurer.co.bw / kfgofhamodimo@atvadventurer.co.bw

Sunrise over the Makgadikgadi Pans.